ADVANCE PRAISE FOR *PRICE PAID*

"A timely tome. So much of Native Canadian history has been swept under the rug by mainstream historians. Fortunately, books like this, written by Native authors themselves, are finally coming out of the closet, so to speak. And the timing couldn't be better. Our country so needs these books. Our country so needs these voices."

—TOMSON HIGHWAY

"By beginning to unveil some painful truths in Canada's 'hidden history,' Chief Bev Sellars provides context and deep understanding that remain at the root of the troubled relationship between Canada and Aboriginal peoples. Some individuals will find these stories troubling, but as painful as these stories are, they must be told if we are to ever have reconciliation and understanding between Aboriginal and non-Aboriginal Canadians."

—MARY SIMON
    co-chair, Canadians for a New Partnership, former Canadian
        ambassador, and president of Inuit Tapiriit Kanatami One

"Reconciliation between Aboriginal and non-Aboriginal peoples in Canada will advance only when non-Aboriginal Canadians learn, accept, remember, and respect Aboriginal perspectives and interpretations of our shared past and future. Bev Sellars's powerful truth-telling about the cost to Aboriginal peoples of our history is essential reading for all Canadians."

—PHYLLIS SENESE
    Professor Emerita of History, University of Victoria

"Sellars uses a broad brush with personal detail here and there to help readers understand Aboriginal issues in Canada today ... a good primer."

—CHRIS ARNETT
    author of *The Terror of the Coast: Land Alienation and Colonial War
    on Vancouver Island and the Gulf Islands, 1849–1863*

PRICE PAID
THE FIGHT FOR FIRST NATIONS SURVIVAL

This book tells the story of the struggle to defend Aboriginal lands, resources, and cultures from first contact until the present. It fills in omitted story segments, corrects stories that are inaccurate, and tells history from a First Nations point of view. Interwoven with personal experiences of indigenous governance, and with a foreword and excerpts by Hemas Kla-Lee-Lee-Kla (Hereditary Chief Bill Wilson), *Price Paid* gives us a sense of how Aboriginal people have managed under the notorious and capricious Indian Act.

For nearly three decades, Bev Sellars has spoken out on behalf of her community, the Xat'súll (Soda Creek) First Nation in Williams Lake, British Columbia, bringing attention to racism and residential schools and to environmental and social threats of mineral resource exploitation in her region.

Her first book, *They Called Me Number One: Secrets and Survival at an Indian Residential School*, spent more than forty weeks on the B.C. bestsellers list. It won the 2014 George Ryga Award for Social Awareness in Literature; third prize in the 2014 Burt Award for First Nations, Métis, and Inuit Literature; and was shortlisted for the 2014 Hubert Evans Non-Fiction Prize.

PRAISE FOR BEV SELLARS'S PREVIOUS BOOK
THEY CALLED ME NUMBER ONE

"Sellars's memoir celebrates the triumph of returning from the brink, it is also a stark condemnation of historical and extant paternalistic policies and the personal tragedies these policies continue to breed."
— *CANADIAN LITERATURE*

"Deeply personal, sorrowful and ultimately triumphal, *They Called Me Number One* is an important addition to the literature on residential schools, and Canada's reckoning with its colonial past."
— *WINNIPEG FREE PRESS*

"*They Called Me Number One* is from my perspective necessary reading across the generations ... a book that speaks honestly and straightforwardly to the residential school experience in British Columbia and in Canada."
—JEAN BARMAN

PRICE PAID

The Fight for First Nations Survival

BEV SELLARS

Foreword and Excerpts by
HEMAS KLA-LEE-LEE-KLA
(Hereditary Chief Bill Wilson)

Talonbooks

Talonbooks
278 East First Avenue, Vancouver, British Columbia, Canada V5T 1A6
www.talonbooks.com

First printing: 2016

Typeset in Warnock
Printed and bound in Canada on 100% post-consumer recycled paper

Interior and cover design by Typesmith
Cover image is a poster for the Maurice Bulbulian film *Dancing Around the Table* © 1987 National Film Board of Canada. Used by permission National Film Board of Canada

Talonbooks acknowledges the financial support of the Canada Council for the Arts, the Government of Canada through the Canada Book Fund, and the Province of British Columbia through the British Columbia Arts Council and the Book Publishing Tax Credit.

LIBRARY AND ARCHIVES CANADA CATALOGUING IN PUBLICATION

Sellars, Bev, 1955–, author
Price paid : the fight for First Nations survival / Bev Sellars ; foreword and excerpts by Hemas Kla-Lee-Lee-Kla (Hereditary Chief Bill Wilson).

Includes bibliographical references and index.
Issued in print and electronic formats.
ISBN 978-0-88922-972-3 (paperback). – ISBN 978-1-77201-098-5 (epub). –
ISBN 978-1-77201-099-2 (kindle). – ISBN 978-1-77201-100-5 (pdf)

1. Indians of North America – Canada – History. 2. Indians of North America – Legal status, laws, etc. – Canada. I. Wilson, Bill, 1944–, writer of foreword II. Title.

E78.C2S3956 2016   971.004'97   C2016-903796-7
                                     C2016-903797-5

To all our ancestors who fought for Aboriginal rights in Canada. The fight to defend our lands, our resources, and our cultures has never ended despite government legislation, depravation, and simple racism. Those of us still here stand on their shoulders to complete the fight for freedom.

I also want to dedicate this book to Hemas Kla-Lee-Lee-Kla (Hereditary Chief Bill Wilson), who taught me and so many others what the fight is really about.

Kukwstéc-kucw (on behalf of all of us, thank you)

History consists of the stories that we tell ourselves about past events. But what happens when a story is incorrectly told or missing altogether? When significant parts are missing, then the story is incomplete and understanding is skewed. If the story is incorrectly told, then our understanding of ourselves is erroneous. However, if there is no story at all, then humanity is denied. We do have opportunities and, we believe, responsibilities to fill in omitted story segments, to correct the stories that are inaccurate, and to include missing stories.

—CORA J. VOYAGEUR, DAVID NEWHOUSE,
AND DAN BEAVON
  Hidden in Plain Sight: Contributions of Aboriginal
  Peoples to Canadian Identity and Culture

We are a people with special rights guaranteed us by promises and treaties. We do not beg for these rights, nor do we thank you ... we do not thank you for them because we paid for them ... and God help us the price we paid was exorbitant. We paid for them with our culture, our dignity, and self-respect. We paid and paid and paid ...

—CHIEF DAN GEORGE

(Geswanouth Slahoot), Tsleil-Waututh Nation

Contents

xiii   Foreword
           by Hemas Kla-Lee-Lee-Kla
             (Hereditary Chief Bill Wilson)

xxi   Preface

xxv   —DECONSTRUCTING NEWCOMER "HISTORY"
           by Jacinda Mack

1   Introduction

         Chapter One
15   **Indian Givers**
         ABORIGINAL CONTRIBUTIONS
         From the Time of Our Ancestors to Contact

         Chapter Two
33   **The Tilting of Power**
         A CLASH OF CULTURES IN THE AMERICAS
         From Contact to the Early Nineteenth Century

         Chapter Three
45   **Case Study in Colonial Contact**
         HISTORY OF THE XAT'SÚLL COMMUNITY
         Early Nineteenth Century to 1876

Chapter Four

61 **Workarounds and Memorials**
EARLY EFFECTS OF THE INDIAN ACT
1876 to 1920s

Chapter Five

81 **Increasing Containment and Repression**
AMENDMENTS TO THE INDIAN ACT
1920s to 1946

Chapter Six

95 **Political Action Renews**
THE INDIAN ACT FROM 1951 FORWARD
1951 to 1969

111 —LEONARD PELTIER IS MY BROTHER
by Hemas Kla-Lee-Lee-Kla
(Hereditary Chief Bill Wilson)

Chapter Seven

117 **Aboriginal Leaders and First Ministers**
CONSTITUTIONAL CONFERENCE
ON ABORIGINAL AFFAIRS
by Hemas Kla-Lee-Lee-Kla
(Hereditary Chief Bill Wilson)
March 15 and 16, 1983

Chapter Eight

129 **The Indian Act and Indian Band Governance**
MY PERSONAL EXPERIENCE
1980s onward

Chapter Nine

149　**Re-establishing Aboriginal Rights**
　　　SUPREME COURT OF CANADA DECISIONS
　　　FROM CALDER TO TSILHQOT'IN
　　　1973 to 2015

Chapter Ten

173　**Realities of Life on the Rez**
　　　THE XAT'SÚLL COMMUNITY TODAY
　　　Present Day

Conclusion

183　**The Tilting of Power Back to First Nations**
　　　A DUTY TO CONSULT
　　　The Future

188　Notes

197　Further Reading

202　Index

209　Acknowledgements

Foreword

HEMAS KLA-LEE-LEE-KLA. This name of rank has been handed down to worthy chiefs for thousands of years. My white name, Bill Wilson, plain and common as it is, has no meaning to my people.

My people are the Kwawkgewlth. We have always been from northern Vancouver Island along the Inside Passage, the Broughton Archipelago, and the mainland inlets. Our home was the sea. Land was a place to build our Big Houses and to tie up our canoes.

My people were a warrior tribe, just as the Haida, who roamed the coast at will. Thousands of years before the first white man stumbled ashore, my people had a complex society based on the potlatch, our form of government. It is from the potlatch that my name came. Worthy men who have proven themselves by accomplishment receive the name as recognition of their right to be a Hamatsa and a chief in our tribe.

My grandfather, Hemas Kla-Lee-Lee-Kla, was the last real Hamatsa. After being nurtured with special foods, training, and care, he was sent out into the wilderness to become one with nature. It was not enough that he had received the best training that humans could provide. He had to be imbued with nature's lessons before he was qualified to be a chief and a leader of his people.

"Oombly," as we called him, was gone in the wilderness for four years without any human contact. He was adopted by wolves and taught to be one with nature. He was told when he left the village that he would receive a sign when he was worthy to come back to lead his people. The sign came in the form of a huge creature with green eyes that appeared on top of a deadfall under which Oombly was sleeping. The creature jumped down and landed on Oombly's chest without hurting him in any way. The creature signalled to Oombly to follow him. They ran and swam back to his village, where the potlatch had been prepared for his return and initiation as a Hamatsa.

The creature stood with Oombly on the rock ridge above the Big House where the potlatch had begun. The creature jumped to the roof of the Big House and then disappeared through the smoke hole into the fire. Hearing human voices for the first time in four years, Oombly started to feel as a human. He was afraid that he would break his legs if he jumped the long distance to the Big House roof. Just then the creature re-appeared at his side and took him by the arm. Together they jumped to the Big House roof and through the smoke hole into the fire. He was back. His brothers and other handlers pulled him from the fire and in a series of four dances he was tamed and became the half human, half animal chief now fully worthy of leadership. Oombly was now Hemas Kla-Lee-Lee-Kla.

I remember my grandfather. I was about six years old when he died. It would have been 1950 when he passed away at age eighty-nine. Just think, he had been born only three years after British Columbia was named, some ten years before we became a province. In an arranged marriage, he had taken a bride. The marriage was sanctified in a potlatch. His wife, Adana, was a full-grown woman before she even saw her first white man, such was the isolation of the land and sea that my people called home. But the paradise we called home was soon to be adulterated.

THE FIRST WHITE men were the missionaries. My grandfather had the potlatch as his religion and was just amused by the Christians. When I was about five years old, I was seated on Oombly's lap watching some of the people in Kingcome march to the little church at the other end of the village. I guess it was a Sunday but

I didn't know or care. I sat on my grandfather's lap, being serviced by his slaves, content in the knowledge that because of him I was protected, well-fed, warm, and happy.

My grandfather explained Christianity to me. He said that the white man had only one god while our people had many gods because of all the work that needed to be done. He said that the white man's god must be a very angry one because they kept him locked up in that little white house and only visited him once in a while. Our gods were everywhere, he said, in the air, the sea, the mountains, and the land.

I loved sitting in Oombly's lap. He always smelled of smoke even though he didn't use tobacco. He smelled of smoke because he always tended the smokehouse, which he did not trust to his slaves. He was the "expert" at smoking salmon and he did not want his people to receive anything but the best. That was the nature of his chieftainship. Despite his high rank, he was the poorest person in the village. It was his job to provide for his people. Only after they had taken their share could he take his. Service to his people was his purpose in life. Hemas means "the Chief who is always there to help." Kla-Lee-Lee-Kla means "the first rank among the eagles." It is from Oombly that my family and I are descended. We did not need the Indian Act or any white recognition to know who we were.

The potlatch, our system of government, was outlawed by the Canadian government in 1884. The Christians were not doing well in our and other areas. The John A. Macdonald government passed the law to outlaw the potlatch in an effort to make Indians Christians. This law was applied in our area with little effect. It served only to drive the potlatch underground and as "a forbidden fruit" it became more attractive to my people.

The potlatch flourished until my people were "sold out" by two weaklings who accepted government money to trap the real chiefs. With the dirty money provided by the federal government, my grandfather and other chiefs were arrested on Village Island for participating in a potlatch. Oombly spent six months behind bars at the Oakalla Prison Farm in Burnaby. He and his people refused to eat the white man's food. My people paddled from Kingcome Inlet with canoes full of "Indian food" to feed our chiefs. They paddled down the coast to the Fraser River, upstream to a place near Oakalla, and then they walked over the hill to the prison farm. There they would feed our chiefs through the metal fence before going home for more food.

My mother, Puugladee, was the oldest child of Oombly and Adana. Two girls followed, causing Oombly to deem my mother a man in order for her to inherit and pass on his songs, dances, names, regalia, and traditions. She was treated by our people as a person of high rank in the potlatch. She always said that the potlatch was her life and she proved it by hosting at least six of these expensive gatherings. Even after moving to the Comox Valley, she participated in every potlatch in every village.

Ethel was my mother's white name. Everyone called her "Effery." She had inherited her father's strength and dignity. She was fluent in Kwakwala (our language) and English having read every book that she could get her hands on. Mom raised at least seventeen kids, five from my father's first marriage to a Lummi Indian lady, six of her own, and half a dozen adopted cousins. I was the youngest of the lot and like my grandfather I was raised to be a chief.

MY FATHER, CHARLIE Wilson, was born and raised just north of Seymour Narrows, site of the famous Ripple Rock detonation in 1958. His father died when he was only twelve and as the eldest child of six he had to build a home for his mother and family. Work occupied all of his life. He never smoked or drank despite the fact that he had lots of money and could do anything that he wanted. When asked why he never drank, Charlie replied that he was always too busy working. As a "commoner" that was his life. He provided well for his huge collected family and his wife's potlatches. He died from the complications of diabetes at sixty-two.

Dad told me a story about the early days of Vancouver Island. He had gone to Vancouver to pick up his new car, there being no car dealership on the island. On the ferry back to Nanaimo he met a young fellow who asked him where Comox was. They were outside on the back deck, the only place that Indians were allowed above the car deck in those days. It turned out that the young man was on his way from England to settle with his uncle in the Comox Valley. My father knew and even employed the man's uncle, who owned a tugboat. My dad offered to drive the young fellow to Comox in his new car. On the way up the island the young passenger kept looking around every time they came to a clearing or meadow. My dad asked him what he was looking for. "Indians" he said excitedly. "What do you think I am?" my dad asked. "Perhaps a Chinese or Japanese," the Englishman said. "No, I am a full-blooded native Indian," my dad said. This hastened the young Englishman to the passenger-side window, where he stayed until they got to Comox. My dad dropped his passenger at the uncle's place. After thanking my dad the young man said in his heavy British accent, "My god, who ever heard of an Indian driving a motor car!"

Dad paid cash for a beautiful home on four and a half acres of property adjacent to the golf course in 1944, the year that I was born. The property came with two indentured servants who my dad freed immediately. We were the first Indian family in the Comox Valley to live off the reserve. My older brothers and sisters suffered the blatant racism extant in the province at the time. My father's money bought us tolerance and we eventually earned respect by our accomplishments in school and athletics. By the time that I got to high school in Courtenay, we were accepted if only as curiosities.

My brother Calvin, who went on to be an ironworker for thirty-three years, told me that when they moved to Courtenay about two years before I was born, he had to fight his way to school every day. He literally had to beat people up to survive. He was mad when they moved to Comox because, in his words, he "had to beat up a whole new crop of racists." But that was 1944, and things could only get better with the war soon ending and people with new experiences coming home to help build a new province.

My mother "Effery" was the cultural strength of our family. She raised us to be Indians in a white man's world. The potlatch was her bible and, even though she exposed us to the Anglican Church, she taught us the real laws of our tribe. I became a Hamatsa and earned my grandfather's name. I did not spend four years in the forest but I did enough to satisfy my mother and the elders that I was fit to become Hemas Kla-Lee-Lee-Kla.

Now at seventy-two, I look back on the past 150 and more years since British Columbia was named. For my people it has been a constant fight that continues today. My people and other tribes built this province despite being marginalized, ignored, trampled upon, incarcerated, abused, and even killed. My reminiscences do not leave me angry even though I have cried to myself in recounting them. Instead, I am proud of my family and their accomplishments. I have one of the highest ranking names in our potlatch. In March of 1983, I helped draft and successfully argue for the entrenchment of the first and only amendment of Canada's new constitution. We have eighteen university degrees in our family and best of all I have five granddaughters who by their strength and breeding will continue to make this province and this country a better place for all of us.

I am especially proud of Bev Sellars, who shares her life with me, and for all she has done to help Canadians understand the experience of Aboriginal people. It is my honour to welcome readers to her book, *Price Paid: The Fight for First Nations Survival.*

WE ARE ALL familiar with the fiction that Columbus discovered America despite the truth that he was lost in the Caribbean only to be saved by the Native people already there.

Many other myths, assumptions, stereotypes, prejudices, sophistries, and outright lies have whitewashed the real history of the continent. Now here is a book that reveals the truth about what really happened here after the immigrants "stumbled ashore."

Bev Sellars begins with the huge contribution made to the world by the Native Indian peoples of North, Central, and South America. She goes on to tell the truth about the relationship between the First Peoples and the newcomers since contact and through the colonial era.

Truth and knowledge are wonderful things. We can all be better informed with Bev's ongoing work.

—HEMAS KLA-LEE-LEE-KLA
Hereditary Chief of the Musgamagw
Chief Bill Wilson, B.A., LL.B.

Preface

I HAVE OFTEN wondered what life would have been like in my community of Soda Creek if newcomers had never arrived. I have heard stories about our ancestors from story keepers in my community. Growing up I learned through oral history instruction stories that tell a completely different view of contact in the Americas. These stories present a history that is not widely known.

As ugly as it may be sometimes, we cannot do a proper job of examining history without looking at the whole picture. We have to peel away the layers of "history" to get people to understand and address the ongoing conflict between Aboriginal and non-Aboriginal communities.

Why should we? Canada projects an international reputation that does not match the reality at home, where on a daily basis Aboriginal Canadians face inequality, lack of education, barriers to employment, and reduced opportunity for self-determination. Not dealing justly with Aboriginal peoples makes Canada no better than the countries Canadians condemn for human rights violations.

Historically politicians have ignored Aboriginal issues because fighting for the rights of First Nations, Inuit, and Metis people, while morally right to do so, would not win votes. My purpose in writing this history of Native-newcomer relations in Canada is to help the Canadian public become more aware of the injustice Aboriginal Canadians live with every day so together we can push our members of Parliament and members of the legislative assembly to resolve these issues. Even though much of this book refers to the area where I live, the history is similar right across Canada. All Aboriginal people have their own stories of struggle in their territories.

BEFORE CANADA WAS a country, the Aboriginal people occupied the land that now bears that name. When the King of England in the Royal Proclamation of 1763 recognized our inherent title to the land, the Proclamation stated that Aboriginal people were not to be "molested or disturbed" in their lands. Territories not already ceded or purchased by the British Crown would be reserved for Aboriginal people and only the British Crown could acquire these lands through treaty negotiations. Treaties were made with the British Crown, establishing the character and reach of Aboriginal rights and title throughout most of Canada, especially on the Prairies. For different reasons, the treaty process was not completed, so today, many parts of Canada still have no treaties for traditional territorial land.

After section 35 of the Constitution Act, 1982, affirmed that Aboriginal title, and the rights that go along with it, exist whether or not there is a treaty, Aboriginal people began to win land claims in the court system across Canada. Eventually the governments realized they needed to deal with this matter. As an example, in 1993 the British Columbia Treaty Commission was set up and the process for negotiating treaties began.

When I worked for the B.C. Treaty Commission from 2003 to 2009 it was part of my employment responsibilities to attend a number of negotiation tables around the province. At the table were representatives of three parties: First Nations and federal and provincial governments gathered to discuss matters relating to Aboriginal rights and title. The B.C. Treaty Commission was "Keeper of the Process" related to negotiations for Aboriginal treaty rights left unresolved when British Columbia joined Confederation in 1871. I quickly realized that many of the negotiators, non-Aboriginal and even some Aboriginal people, had no idea *why* they were negotiating treaties. Too many at the negotiating table did not understand the historic reasons Aboriginal rights and title are still open to negotiation, that Canada has a duty to uphold treaties negotiated with Britain following the Proclamation of 1763. Many treaty negotiators were simply administering government policy. They knew little of the history of this country and even thought that Aboriginal people contributed nothing toward the negotiations. One comment that burned me then and still burns me today was said by a non-Aboriginal negotiator: "B.C. brings land to the negotiation table. Canada brings money. The First Nations do not bring anything to the table." My response is that Aboriginal people bring all the land, and the money the governments bring comes from resources held on Aboriginal lands.

It was then that I decided I needed to develop an information session and educate these newcomers about the history of our country. I asked my non-Aboriginal supervisor about it and was told I could do it off the side of my desk. When Stephen Point, a member of the Stó:lō Nation, became chief commissioner, I spoke directly with him. He agreed that an information session was needed and gave me the go-ahead to develop it.

I used my degrees in history and law and my personal experience growing up on the reserve and in an Indian residential school to design a two-hour presentation telling Canadian history from an Aboriginal point of view. I delivered that presentation in many parts of British Columbia over the next few years. It was well received by both Aboriginal and non-Aboriginal groups. Unfortunately I never was able to break into the circle of non-Aboriginal negotiators – the ones who needed it most. I was, however, invited to present to a number of government ministries.

Former Premier Mike Harcourt was a B.C. Treaty Commissioner at the time and invited me to present at a conference he was hosting. Afterward Mike encouraged me to turn my presentation into a book. He left the commission a while later and I didn't follow up with him. After the success of my first book, *They Called Me Number One*, Talonbooks was looking for another and

I remembered Harcourt's comments. And so the basis of this book is the two-hour presentation expanded and developed with updated information as well as historic detail. The experiences shared in this book fill in some of the gaps in the history of Native-newcomer relations in Canada and correct misunderstandings that will help the reader understand the First Nations fight for survival. This is a personal history but also a community history. It speaks to the history of all Canadians and the responsibility we all share – to resolve conflict between Natives and newcomers, between Aboriginal and non-Aboriginal communities, and to demand equality for Canadians of all backgrounds, especially Canada's First Peoples.

THIS BOOK SHARES MY personal experience of the racism inherent in the Indian Act, which imposed reserve boundaries on lands that cannot support their population. Discussion begins by establishing the significance of some of the contributions Aboriginal people have made to the world and learning about the state of their culture and society pre-contact – so that the reader clearly understands that Aboriginal peoples in Canada went from a position of power to one of subjugation. The book then shows how disease and the clash of cultures between newcomers and Aboriginal people shifted the balance of power. Instead of being given the respect and regard Canadian society should afford its First Peoples, rights were removed by the Indian Act, which, along with other legislation were used to marginalize Indians on reserves and suppress the cultures of Aboriginal people. I show how those laws affected the everyday lives of Aboriginal people right through to 1951 when the Indian Act was somewhat overhauled and the underground fight for Aboriginal survival emerged in the form of blockades, court cases, and political action. Hope for the future of Canada ends the

> I know of no other book that talks about living through the repression of the Indian Act and how it has affected the individual.

book. The historical relationship between Aboriginal people and the newcomers was based on the newcomers' assumption that their customs, culture, language, laws, and religion were superior. This has been the foundation upon which our country was built. It is my intention in this book to trace how this ridiculous attitude has robbed Aboriginal people of basic human rights. I know of no other book that talks about living through the repression of the Indian Act and how it has affected the individual. My purpose in writing a popular history from a personal point of view is to help the reader understand a fuller history of Canada that includes the perspectives of Aboriginal people.

My daughter, Jacinda Mack, shared an experience that highlighted the differences between the ways newcomer "history" is presented and the perspective of Aboriginal people. During her undergraduate studies, she took a course on Northwest Coast history and the material culture of the Aboriginal peoples of what is now known as British Columbia. As part of an assignment, she had to "deconstruct" a historical text. This preface closes with the story Jacinda tells.

DECONSTRUCTING NEWCOMER "HISTORY"

For this history project, I chose to deconstruct a series of photos taken in Bella Coola during the 1920s. The photos showed Aboriginal Nuxalk people posing in traditional attire, including dance blankets, three coppers, and a marriage board (a box cover set with sea otter teeth given by the husband to help his new wife "make teeth"). The Nuxalk men and women were quite striking. To some, they would be referred to nostalgically as "noble savages." I noted that the European people of the same era were photographed in suits or in more casual clothing, but never in ceremonial kilts, for example. My assignment deconstructed the photos as products of salvage ethnography, recasting the "vanishing Indian" myth. These Aboriginal people were "dressed up" for

ORIGINAL CAPTION:
Bella Coola Amerindians in ceremonial regalia, Bella Coola River Valley, B.C.

JACINDA'S CAPTION:
Albert King, Willie Mack, and Eliza Moody, on her wedding day, July 16, 1922

PHOTO by Harlan Ingersoll Smith. Canadian Museum of Civilization, 56909

the purpose of the photo, in ceremonial attire, but presented as an everyday, pre-colonial image.

In the original photo series, the captions gave the full names and titles of only the European men and referred to the Aboriginal people simply as "Bella Coola Indians" or "people in costume." As a descendant of these people, I understood that names are the biggest form of title and culture a person can hold in that part of the world. These people were efficiently silenced, disgraced, belittled, and dismissed by the omission of meaningful photo captions. I chose to turn the tables in order to make visible the subtext of racism and ethnocentric assumptions.

I found out the names of the Nuxalk people by simply asking around the community where the photos had been taken, and living relatives provided me with the information I asked for, nearly a hundred years later. With this simply acquired information, I recaptioned the original 1920s photos with the Aboriginal names, titles, and villages of our Nuxalk nation. I labelled other photos showing European men (the photographers visiting the Aboriginal community), simply as "White Men" with no further information, despite the significant contributions to the anthropological record that their photo series represents.

When I presented the new "text" of the edited photos to my anthropology class, the effect was immediate. Both instructor and students were obviously shocked at the captions; they could not pronounce the Aboriginal names and were upset that the European men were so unceremoniously dismissed, despite their "obvious authority" as creators of the photo series. It was a great learning discussion for most as it questioned many aspects of culture, privilege, and how information is framed and understood.

—JACINDA MACK

Introduction

HISTORICAL DOCUMENTS are the basis for much of our understanding of history, but given my experience I suggest they should be analyzed thoroughly to determine how valid they are. Records can sometimes be distorted depending on the circumstances of the person, the time of writing, and the reasons for recording. There are too many silent voices that somehow have to be included in the equation. A good example of that is the Aboriginal voice.

Anthropologist Wendy Wickwire examines incidents as told by Simon Fraser in the written form and compares them with the same incidents as told by Native people through oral tradition. It is interesting to see what is left out, and to think about why these details are absent from Simon Fraser's journals but told in the oral tradition of the Aboriginal peoples. Wickwire writes: "there are events chronicled in these Native historical accounts that are missing in Fraser's journal – for example, the story about a woman who is fondled by Fraser at the mouth of the Stein. Also new is the fear that the Indians would be 'cleaned out' by disease simply by touching the strangers."

We need to become the explorers of the explorers and government documents. We need to understand that the original message has gone through so much filtration or alteration. What we hear or see today may be completely different from the original incident. I see the transformation from historic moment to history text as vulnerable at any number of missteps, which should be questioned as follows:

ORIGINAL EVENT

↓

Is the source of information a non-Aboriginal speaker or translator?
If so, the message may have changed from one language to another.

↓

Was the message translated into additional other
languages, say from Aboriginal to French to English?

↓

Is this an eyewitness report? Is it hearsay or rumour?

↓

Did the writer have any biases?

↓

Was the event recorded? If so, what did the recorder and the
act of recording bring into the act of record keeping?

↓

For whom were the records written? Would the
audience have affected the telling of the story?

↓

What is the date? place? time of the event?
What were the circumstances?

↓

Were cultural differences taken into account?

↓

Were the original records altered by anyone?

↓

After all this filtration we end up with today's written records.
How accurate are they? These are the questions we need to
ask as we explore historic documents that report the history
of Aboriginal people from the newcomer's point of view.

MY EXPLORATION OF HISTORY began when I first entered
university in my thirties. Attending university had always been my
dream but for a number of reasons I didn't get there. Bill Wilson,
my husband, was born and raised on Vancouver Island and had

completed his bachelor of arts at the University of Victoria (UVic). He suggested I consider applying there. I thought I was too old to go to university, but Bill convinced me that even at the late age of thirty-eight I could attend. Applying as a mature student, I was accepted for enrolment at UVic.

In September 1993, my youngest son, Tony, and I moved from the Soda Creek reserve to Victoria. The culture shock that came with living in a city far from home was tough to take. I wanted to go home to visit my family, especially my increasingly frail grandmother, but Victoria is a city at the southern tip of Vancouver Island. If I wanted to leave on a long weekend or holiday, so did many other people. Tony and I spent long hours waiting our turn to board the ferries to the mainland.

That first year at university, like most students I had no idea what my major would be. I signed up for four courses but needed one more to make up a full course load, but all the courses I wanted were over-registered. The only one that fit my schedule was history and I had no desire to take that. All the history textbooks we had used in high school and that my children brought home ignored Aboriginal history or treated it as almost meaningless.

The first newcomers to the land, the English and the French, had created their own versions of history. I grew up hearing all the stereotypes: that Aboriginal people live on welfare; they pay no government tax; they are dirty, drunk, lazy, or stupid. But I knew otherwise. I knew that much of what was said about Aboriginal people wasn't true. My grandmother told me many stories of the ways she and the generations before her had shared skills and knowledge the newcomers needed when they first came to this land. My grandmother told me stories of the first newcomers she saw as a child in her home community of Alexandria. She said many of them wandered the roads and her dad would sometimes help them with food or temporary shelter. None stayed long and Gram found them a curiosity. Later when my grandmother married and moved to Deep Creek she told stories of our people helping many of the newcomers. I knew from these stories that newcomer "history" told only one version of history.

I reluctantly signed up for the Canadian history course. I wasn't looking forward to four months of the inaccuracies put forward as history but knew I had to suck it up to get the three credits. In our first class, when the professor, Phyllis Senese, started to speak, I knew that something was different. For the first time in my life, I heard an educator talking about history *before* the newcomers arrived. Dr. Senese lectured for two weeks before getting into colonial Canadian history. I was amazed.

That Canadian history course helped me fill in some of the missing stories I knew existed. I went on to discover other courses with Aboriginal content and also took some European and world history courses. Having been educated at an Indian residential school and living on an Indian reserve, I had a limited view of how other countries had developed. Studying history opened up a new way of thinking for me. European history was definitely an eye-opener. I ended up majoring in history and minoring in political science.

AFTER COMPLETING MY undergraduate degree, in September 1998, I thought about going on to do a Ph.D. in history but listened to the advice of others and began classes at the University of British Columbia law school instead. Toward the end of the first month at law school my brother Mike was transferred to Vancouver General Hospital with stab wounds. He had been living on the streets in Williams Lake and got into a dispute with someone. I was the only family member in Vancouver at the time and had to go so I could report on Mike's condition to Mom and the rest of the family back home. I dreaded the visit because I had visions that I would be the only one with Mike when he died. Nevertheless I drove to the hospital late that night and stayed with Mike overnight. He didn't respond when I talked to him and I wasn't given too much hope for his survival. I spent the next few days at my brother's side. That week I didn't go to class or do any of the readings.

My priority was my big brother, my protector. I phoned home on a regular basis to let the family know the status of his condition. Nothing changed for the first few days but one day I went in and the nurse was excited. She said that Mike had opened one eye and seemed to follow her movement around the hospital room. I went and talked to Mike but still no response. It wasn't long after that I went back for another visit and Mike's eyes were open. It took him a while to be able to talk but eventually he did come around and went home to Williams Lake.

In the meantime I had lost a lot of time at law school and was wondering how I would catch up. Through my friends I discovered condensed annotated notes or CANS, which are summaries of all the legal cases you need to know. I wrote my own CANS and got through my Christmas exams, didn't fail any courses, and actually surprised myself at how well I did considering my lack of attendance.

In my second term at law school my husband, Bill, ended up in the hospital. Bill had been living in a small apartment in the heart of Vancouver while I lived with my two sons and a nephew in family housing on campus, a fifteen-minute drive away. Scott, my oldest son, was going to UBC as well, and my younger son, Tony, and my nephew Buck (Gordon) were in grade twelve at the local high school. Bill was working for the Assembly of First Nations while I attended law school, and we saw each other regularly. One evening I got a call from Bill asking me to come down to the apartment. I knew Bill had been sick with the flu but that he was up and around and hadn't gone to see a doctor. When I arrived at the apartment I found Bill on the floor by the bathroom. It couldn't be the flu. He was so weak from vomiting and diarrhea that even sitting up made him almost pass out. I called the ambulance and he was transported the few blocks to St. Paul's Hospital. Apparently he had one huge ulcer and other smaller ones. Bill pulled through but again I lost a lot of time at law school looking after him until he was strong once again.

My law studies simply were not my priority. When a very good friend was losing her husband, I again missed classes after spending an emotional time with her at the hospital before her husband died. For end-of-term exams I used CANS and again did fairly well. Walking out of the law school after my final exam that April, I felt such an immense sense of accomplishment that I gave a victory holler! I had completed my first year of law school despite all the time I had spent at hospitals.

Over the summer I reflected on my first year and realized that I really didn't need to attend classes to get through law school. In second year, the only classes I went to were seminars where attendance and participation made up a big part of the final mark. I enjoyed them, especially the Analysis of Evidence seminar, where we combed over the evidence of a murder and put a case together. Maybe I should have been a detective.

Mainly, though, I didn't find the law interesting; maybe it was amusing at times. When I was prepared for class and had read the case, I was bored with the discussion. If I wasn't prepared and hadn't read the case, I was lost. Either way, I didn't want to be there. Like many Aboriginal people who go to law school, I struggled with the concepts put forward. Some courses like Property Law downright offended me, mainly because I knew the newcomers had violated their own laws; they had never legitimately obtained title to the land. The newcomers' legal system simply imposes laws from across the oceans. The newcomers' culture is based on a feudal system that has no basis in human rights and give no consideration for anyone other than nobility. So rather than endure sitting through discussions I didn't agree with, I stayed away.

One day I decided to go to class mostly to visit my friends and see whether I was missing anything important. I was early and a bit surprised when my friends came in and a couple of them said, "Bev, what are you doing here?" When the professor came in and said the same thing, I chuckled and realized how many classes I missed.

Bryan Williams, QC, former president of the Canadian Bar Association and later chief justice of the Supreme Court of British

Columbia, had been one of our lawyers in the early 1990s for the Cariboo-Chilcotin Justice Inquiry. The inquiry was convened when Native people belonging to the fifteen Indian bands in the area complained about how they were being treated by the justice system, from Royal Canadian Mounted Police enforcement right up to the Supreme Court of British Columbia. I got to know Bryan through Bill, whose older brother Cal grew up with Bryan in Comox. Bill brought me to meet Bryan when we were organizing lawyers to defend our position in the inquiry. We hired him, and Bryan and our team worked well together.

About a year after I finished law school, Bill and I had lunch with Bryan, who asked me about articling. I told him I wasn't interested. Bryan insisted that I should article before making up my mind about a law career; he knew of an articling position available at Miller Thomson LLP and he arranged for me to fill it. I really appreciated that experience and worked with some great people, but articling confirmed that a legal career wasn't for me. I let the partners know months before my term was up that I would not be staying on at Miller Thomson.

I am not discouraging Aboriginal people from studying law. The many Aboriginal lawyers today continue to work for change from inside that discipline. I am only saying that a legal career wasn't for *me*. I should have done a Ph.D. in history, the discipline I had discovered I really enjoyed.

THE LAW DEGREE and articling weren't a waste of four years. They allowed me to refine my research skills to pull all kinds of research together in the analysis of evidence. They were a great education and helped me further understand how the newcomers had set up government and claimed lands across Canada under the Doctrine of Discovery, all the while violating their own English common law and the Crown's policies applicable to Aboriginal nations. Aboriginal people never consented to this. Despite treaty rights initiated in the Proclamation of 1763, racist colonial laws violated our rights, which were continually further eroded through the Indian Act and other federal policies.

The Crown has actively denied Aboriginal rights in countless ways that need to be known. Leaders were thrown in jail; lawyers were banned when court action was organized; laws were imposed to segregate Aboriginal people on reserves, keeping us out of sight and out of mind. This history needs to be known and understood so that a more equitable society can be made available to all Canadians, and that includes First Nations, Inuit, and Metis peoples.

Many Canadians do not know the full history of this country. For example, when I was articling at Miller Thomson I went to lunch with a bunch of articling students. We were sitting talking and the conversation got around to where everyone had come from. The one young lady said something like, "Everyone in Canada came from somewhere else." I was a little stunned to hear her say this and another woman quickly informed her that, "Bev doesn't come from another country. She is Aboriginal." The young woman was quite shocked at this information. I later wondered what the conversation around her dinner table was that night. Like many people uninformed about Aboriginal people, she had not thought about the prior existence of the First Peoples in Canada. An older man at UVic when I was giving a presentation there said to me, "I was educated in the university system and I consider myself well read. How is it that at my age I knew nothing about the residential schools?"

I got a phone call after my first book came out from a white woman who was exactly my age. She said that she knew nothing of residential schools and it really disturbed her that while I was going to the residential schools and being subject to laws under the Indian Act that she was enjoying everything that Canada had to offer. She had attended a public school and her parents were fully involved with her education. She compared my life to hers year for year. She was very upset that in a country that allowed her to have so much, the First Peoples of this land were denied. She apologized for all that I had been through because of her ancestors. I told her as I have told countless others who have apologized to me over the years, "I know you are not personally responsible for these laws and policies, but now that you are aware, you have a responsibility to help change the situation. You cannot turn a blind eye to this because, if you do, you will be doing the same thing as your ancestors." That would be my message to all Canadians. Her call meant a lot to me because she had taken the time to learn of the Canadian history that had been hidden from her. Without awareness among all Canadians, we cannot build a better society.

POVERTY AND LACK of opportunity are impediments to Aboriginal achievement but endemic to a racially discriminatory set of laws and policies at the federal level. I know about poverty. I have been involved with my community all my life. I served as the elected chief for twelve years, first taking office in 1987. Even when I was away at university, my thoughts were always about my home community. I wanted to learn new skills to help with the struggle we were in.

My community is a stereotypical example of an Aboriginal community in Canada. We are not prosperous but we do get by. More than half the people in our community are unable to secure permanent employment. We lack sufficient educational funds to send our children off for higher learning. The minimum funds we are able to provide are insufficient to allow our students to study free of constant concern that they need to pay the bills. I was fortunate that my credit rating was good when I went to university as a mature student. I was able to get student loans and after seven years had accumulated $40,000 in debt. I was one of the lucky ones. Most Aboriginal students in this country cannot afford, and are not provided with the opportunity, to go on to any form of higher learning. I bristle when I hear non-Aboriginal people say that Indians get a free education. It is as wrong as those who say we do not pay taxes – while everyone else in the country profits from resources extracted on our territorial lands. Most "Indian" people pay the same taxes as everyone else. I am still looking for the imaginary reserve that provides everything for free. I am a status Indian living on reserve and get very few tax breaks. Like most of the more than three thousand Indian reservations in Canada, we do not have a store or gas station in our community. If I want a small tax break on gas, I have to travel a fair distance for it. I don't smoke so the break I get to kill myself with lung cancer is of no use to me. I do 99.9 percent of my shopping off-reserve and pay the same sales taxes as anyone else.

It would be wonderful if the taxes we all pay went toward maintaining the infrastructure. This, unfortunately, is not the case. If you were to travel to my reserve, you would know right away when you hit the rez by the quality of the roads. It is paved right to the boundary of the reserve and then a washboard, dirt road takes over through the rez. This is common on most reserves and it gets worse – in many cases across Canada Indian reserves do not even have clean water to drink. Houses are poorly constructed and in decay.

There is no mystery about why most reserves are pockets of poverty. Reserves are like factories that the Department of Indian Affairs operates. At one end of the conveyor belt, government allocates billions of dollars to the Department of Indian Affairs. A huge chunk of the money gets diverted off to pay the salaries of mostly non-Aboriginal people in big office towers in cities. Hundreds of millions of dollars keep travelling down the conveyor belt as the Department of Indian Affairs decides where to shovel money to ease our suffering – from education funding to economic development plans – yet Aboriginal people continue to live in poverty. The end product of the factory is very little because no product is expected.

THE ISSUES ABORIGINAL PEOPLE FACE across Canada are similar. The after-effects of colonialism and residential schools are evident. The loss of our traditional lands, loss of our own decision-making ability, and government underfunding in our communities have taken their toll. It is clear to me that several structural problems stand in the way of Aboriginal peoples – problems entrenched in Canada's constitution, laws, and culture and rooted in the Indian Act, which was drafted in 1876.

It is absolutely essential that Canadians understand the containment the Indian Act represents, how Aboriginal people fought back against its restrictions, how this history came about, what happened, and why. Aboriginal peoples were here to meet the first newcomers to this land and we continue to welcome them today despite continued oppression. I was proud to see some Aboriginal communities step up recently to help welcome the Syrian refugees in Prince Albert, Saskatchewan, and Roseau River, Manitoba. I believe that Aboriginal peoples can relate to the suffering refugees experience and that is why, when we can, we are still helping newcomers today.

It is the assumption of superiority on which this country's history has been based that must change. A society will never achieve its full potential unless all members can exercise their human rights and achieve their full potential.

WHAT IF YOU OWNED A HOUSE AND BEAUTIFUL GARDEN? WOULD YOU SHARE IT WITH OTHERS? WOULD YOU WELCOME THEM?

40,000 YEARS AGO

Human habitation begins in the Americas

4,000 YEARS AGO

Secwepemc occupy territory at Soda Creek

1400S

Population of the Americas estimated at between 90 and 112.5 million

Chapter One

Indian Givers

ABORIGINAL CONTRIBUTIONS

From the Time of Our Ancestors to Contact

ABORIGINAL PEOPLE IN the Americas have shared our wealth with the rest of the world. When I delivered my two-hour presentation, I titled the first section "Indian Givers" after the title of a book by anthropologist Jack Weatherford. The first slide listed titles of the five sections I would be presenting. If I was talking to an Aboriginal audience, I would hear groans when people started filing into the room and saw the title on the first slide.

The Indian givers concept has taken on a negative connotation over the years. "Indian givers" usually refers to someone gifting something and then taking it back. But I would tell my Aboriginal audiences, "By the time I am finished my presentation you will be very proud to be an Indian giver." I also encouraged them to change the language we use to describe ourselves.

Etymologist David Wilton says the concept of an "Indian gift" arose when newcomers misinterpreted the Aboriginal practice of bartering. Wilton identified that, for Aboriginal people, the giving of gifts was simply another form of trade and "a gift was expected to be reciprocated with something of equal value. Europeans, upon encountering this practice, misunderstood it, considering it uncouth and impolite. To them, trade was conducted with money and gifts were freely given with nothing expected in return. So this Aboriginal practice got a bad reputation among the newcomers to North America and the term eventually became a playground insult.

As "Indian givers," Aboriginal people have provided to the world many everyday things we now take for granted. Once you know the many contributions of Aboriginal people, you will realize the genius of our Aboriginal ancestors.

ABORIGINAL PEOPLE HAVE been here for thousands of years. Artifacts such as arrowheads, cooking tools, and pit houses found at our community heritage site in Soda Creek, British Columbia, date back four thousand years. Artifacts found in other parts of the Americas date back a lot longer than that, possibly as early as 40,000 BCE.

When the newcomers first came from Europe, Aboriginal people occupied the Americas from the North Pole to Cape Horn. Some estimates put the number of Aboriginal people in North, Central, and South America between 90 and 112.5 million. Each Aboriginal group, from the Inuit in what today is Nunavut to the Yaghan in Tierra del Fuego, were strong, solid, and secure in their culture. They followed strict codes of conduct that governed every aspect of their lives. Births, deaths, marriages, land use, songs, dances, conflicts, and all personal matters were governed by sacred ceremonies that had existed for thousands of years.

Aboriginal societies engaged in an economy that respected the land and all its bounty, from the plants that grow in the earth to the animals that walk in the forests and the fish that swim in the waters. Over thousands of years of life in the Americas, we had developed an intimate knowledge of the land that led to thriving economies because we cared for and nurtured our world. Aboriginal people had lived in and cultivated the lands in the Americas to a degree of richness that still appeals to people around the world today. Our traditional belief is that we borrow the earth from our grandchildren and that we have to keep it healthy for seven generations ahead. It is common practice when we harvest anything from the forest to thank Mother Earth for providing the medicines and plants we need to survive. When we take an animal for food, we offer thanks to the animal for giving its life to feed us. Traditionally we were taught to take only what we needed and to use everything we took. We were taught that, if we take care of Mother Earth, it would take care of us.

When Aboriginal people pray, we usually end with the words *All my relations*. Our relations do not include just our families, they include all humans, all sea creatures, all animals, all plants, and as one elder said, "Even the rocks." Aboriginal people and many others now know that everything is connected, and to disturb one area of the environment is to disturb many other parts as well. With climate change, many people have begun to understand the importance of our relationship to the land and water.

When the newcomers came to the Americas, we freely and generously shared what we knew of the land to help the newly arrived adapt to and overcome the hardships of life here. We shared a wealth of intelligence that was returned to Europe with the explorers who "discovered" America. Today people around the world enjoy certain foods, languages, and medicines without being aware of their origin. Aboriginal people have contributed to the world economy, introduced new sports, improved transportation, strengthened military strategy and government, and inspired art and architecture.

TWO OF OUR MOST significant contributions are silver and gold. The mountain with the richest silver ore deposit ever discovered is Potosí, perched in the Bolivian Mountains of South America. When I went to Lima, Peru, in 2013 and met with Aboriginal people from ten South American countries as part of the Latin American Observatory of Mining Conflicts (OCTAL by its initials in Spanish), the Aboriginal people from Bolivia knew exactly which mountain I was asking about. It was a treat to speak with Aboriginal people who knew the history and could share their stories with me. Some claim they could have built a bridge across the ocean from South America to Spain with the silver extracted from Potosí. The Aboriginal people of Mexico's Guanajuato and Zacatecas, two other silver mines of historic significance in the sixteenth and seventeenth centuries, would share similar stories, I'm sure. The silver that originated in their resource-rich territories was traded not only in Europe but in Ming Dynasty China, inspiring trade routes around the world.

Gold was equally important. The Aboriginal peoples of South America had collected a wealth of golden treasure over centuries of mining and metallurgy. The first flood of new gold into Europe came as a result of the Spanish seizing the accumulated wealth of the Aztec in what is now Mexico, the Muisca in Colombia, and the Incas in Peru. Gold mining then became an obsession as newcomers tried to find *El Dorado*, the fabled land where, after the king bathed each morning, servants would adorn his body with gold dust until he shone like the sun.

All the gold and silver coming from the Americas allowed individuals to break free of royalty and become independent with their own wealth.

IN THEIR PURSUIT of silver and gold, newcomers discovered many other riches, including new foods like corn, beans of all kinds, and squash. Aboriginal people introduced Europeans and the rest of the world to whole new families of foods: potatoes and tomatoes; green, yellow, and red peppers; zucchini, papaya, and pumpkins; peanuts, pecans, and chocolate; avocados, vanilla, chilies, and paprika; cranberries, maple syrup, wild rice, chewing gum, sunflower seeds, and more. This bounty of food crops was taken to Europe from the Americas and it changed world cuisine forever.

I sometimes get a kick out of restaurants that list "traditional" dishes of a certain country when almost always they include traditional foods from the Americas. For example, for more than two thousand years clambakes have been a tradition among communities in parts of North America now known as Massachusetts, Maine, and Connecticut. They cooked clams and lobsters in sand pits, and remnants of historic cooking pits can still be found in

Rhode Island. Yet the Boston Clambake made famous by the new-comers has now spread to other parts of the world.

Newcomers also are given credit for a few other foods that originated in the Americas. Italians claim tomatoes as their own but they actually knew nothing of this fruit before contact with the Americas. There are many theories of how the first tomato reached Italy. The Italians, of course, may have taken the tomato and cross-pollinated plants to develop new versions of tomatoes but the fact is that tomatoes did not originate in Italy. They first grew in the Americas.

The Swiss or Belgians are considered to be the inventors of luxurious sweet chocolate – misinformation proudly shared with me by a young exchange student from Switzerland I was very fortunate to be able to work with in Vancouver in the early 2000s. As we were talking one day, she informed me that the Swiss invented chocolate. I knew that wasn't true and told her that chocolate came from the Aboriginal people of Central America and suggested she look it up on the Internet. I felt bad for her when, national pride deflated, she came back the next day and confirmed what I had told her. She had been raised with the myth that Swiss people were inventors of chocolate. Granted they make fabulous chocolate now but, again, chocolate did not originate in Europe.

The Irish are strongly associated with the potato, but Aboriginal people grew hundreds and some say thousands of different types of potatoes, from varieties for the lowlands to those for the highlands, as well as varieties for cold weather or warm weather and for different types of soils. Unfortunately the Irish did not learn from the Aboriginal people how to cultivate this plant once it was transplanted to Ireland; the result was the Irish potato blight and the famine that occurred when their potatoes were ravaged by disease.

Corn was a very important crop for the Aboriginal people; however, it was never adopted in Europe as readily as the potato. Instead corn was used to feed animals in Europe. Farmers could grow more corn on one acre than grain crops would produce. The animals fed on corn became fat and healthy and the humans who ate the animals also became healthier.

With the introduction of corn, potatoes, and other American crops, the European population exploded. Before contact all empires in Europe and the East, from Greece and Rome to Persia and Egypt, had based success on their control of grain production. These empires, situated in the warmer southern countries where it was easier to grow grain crops, provided colder northern countries with food. Following the introduction of Aboriginal food crops such as the potato, northern countries such as Germany and Russia rose as world powers because they had gained an independent food supply.

OTHER PLANT-BASED CONTRIBUTIONS from the Americas had equally significant economic consequence. Two – cotton and rubber – were important to the Industrial Revolution.

Thousands of years before Charles Goodyear patented a process that strengthens rubber, Meso-American peoples used a similar process to transform latex from the native *Castilla elastica* tree into rubber goods for a variety of uses. MIT researchers show that Meso-Americans, a culture that flourished in what is now Mexico and Central America from at least 2,000 BCE to the Spanish invasion in 1521, produced rubber. Written records of the Spanish conquistadors indicate that these Aboriginal people wore rubber footwear. Archaeologists have found rubber balls, rubber bindings to tie a stone axe head to its wooden handle, moulded rubber figurines, and evidence of rubber adhesives.

When rubber was first encountered by the newcomers, the Europeans viewed the material as a curiosity but quickly forgot it in their search for gold, silver, tobacco, and other profitable products. But with the Industrial Revolution two centuries later, rubber became important for everything from hoses, belts, matting, flooring, footwear, all the way to pencil erasers. Think of all that would not exist if we did not have rubber. Eventually newcomers started rubber plantations in other parts of the world and its use spread, especially with the twentieth-century invention of the automobile and bicycle and their use of rubber tires. Even though the rubber tree is native to South America and experimentation with latex from its sap was developed by Aboriginals before contact, the reason Charles Goodyear's name is associated with rubber today is that in 1844 he registered with the U.S. Patent Office the vulcanization process that makes rubber more durable.

Cotton from the Americas also brought important economic change during the Industrial Revolution. The large supply of raw cotton transformed European society. American cotton had longer fibres and so was stronger than cotton available from other parts of the world. Manufacture of machines for spinning threads and weaving cotton into fabric began an industrialization process in Europe that over time developed factories for other goods and attracted rural workers into urban centres, increased mobility, liberated them from class structures, and improved health and well being. Cotton improved health around the world because people now had a regular change of clothing.

In addition, the "dirty Indians" of the Americas showed Europeans the benefits of sweats or bathhouses. The Spanish were horrified when they first arrived to see the Aboriginal people bathing on a regular basis. The Spanish believed that disturbing body oils by washing would allow sickness in, and so they bathed on a very limited basis and wore perfume to cover up the smell of their unwashed bodies.

PLANTS WITH MEDICINAL value are other important Aboriginal contributions. Jacques Cartier and his men became ill with scurvy while ice-locked at Stadacona (now Quebec City) during the winter of his second voyage in 1535. It is well documented that the Aboriginal people knew of this disease and showed Cartier how to cure himself and his men with ascorbic acid (vitamin C) decocted by boiling needles and bark from the white spruce tree.

In contrast, medicine in some parts of the world at this time had not risen above placing leeches on a sick person. The history books talk about George Washington, the first president of the United States, dying of a throat infection but it is more likely he died of blood letting. Since the European belief was that the bad stuff was in the blood, they took from him several pints of blood in a twenty-four-hour period. Blood banks today counsel donors not to give more than one pint every two months and *only* if we are well. George Washington probably would have recovered from the throat infection if they had not bled him.

Meanwhile Aboriginal peoples have always used the natural world to cure illnesses, and many of the medicines, ointments, and salves we use today originally came from Aboriginal people. Aboriginal peoples still gather and use these medicines. Many of our people make the yearly pilgrimage in the spring to gather pitch from certain trees for medicine. We boil it and make a liquid drink; we make an ointment used for burns, cuts, and other skin abrasions; and we use a certain type of pitch as a chewing gum. All have great healing properties.

For example, several years ago, it seemed everywhere I looked rosehip extract was being advertised. At the time I thought, "Wow, someone has discovered a new product." I was impressed and determined to try these rosehips so I bought some as part of a vitamin supplement. A while later I went to a community event at Sugar Cane, a neighbouring Aboriginal village, where an elderly lady, Roberta "Birdie" Gilbert, had her usual table full of plants and medicines that she collected on an annual basis. I went over to say hi to Birdie. On one table she had displayed something I knew in our Secwepemc language as *Sekwew* — but Birdie's sign read Rosehips. I had been eating *Sekwew* all my life and knew the medicinal qualities of the berry. Dried, we used it to make tea; fresh, we ate the skin of the berries because of its nice flavour. I knew not to eat the seeds because as the elders warned us, "It will make your bum itchy!" I exclaimed to Birdie, "*That's* what rosehips are? Rosehips are *Sekwew*?" I told Birdie my little story and we both laughed at my ignorance.

Bill has a story told to him by his mother, Puugladee, also known as Ethel Pearson. Bill says: "Hemas Kla-Lee-Lee-Kla, my grandfather after whom I am named, was injured taking planks from trees. A wedge gave way and took the skin and flesh off his left shoulder. His wound was dressed and his injury was not debilitating but sadly the wound became infected and this big man was poisoned in his blood. The elders gathered and examined him and the wound that apparently reeked of decay. They went into the forest and gathered moss and wrapped Hemas's shoulder in the moss. Within a week the infection was gone and Hemas recovered to his full capacity. The non-Aboriginal world now knows this as penicillin. The Aboriginal people knew of it a thousand years before."

It is this kind of story that demonstrates the wealth of plant knowledge Aboriginal people had accumulated from their life on the land. After contact Aboriginal people shared our knowledge of these and other plant-based cures with the newcomers. In fact, by 1820, the United States Pharmacopeia listed more than two hundred medicines and drugs that had originated with Aboriginal people. Researchers today are still collecting medicines used by Aboriginal people. These newcomers may have renamed some of the plants and marketed them under new names, but all of the plants were already in use.

Unfortunately, the Aboriginal people had no medicines for diseases the newcomers brought with them. From the early seventeenth to the mid-nineteenth century, when forts and fur-trading posts were established across North America, Aboriginal people came into close contact with the newcomers and epidemics of smallpox and other diseases ravaged Aboriginal populations.

IN OUR AREA, the Cariboo region of British Columbia, first contact took place 1793, when Alexander Mackenzie trekked through on his way to the sea. When Simon Fraser explored our territory in 1808, Secwepemc people shared our food and guided him by canoe on the Upper Fraser River. When Fort Alexandria was built in 1821, we supplied salmon, meat, berries, roots, and pitch for repairing canoes. In eastern North America, Aboriginal people supplied the forts with corn, maple sugar, wild rice, buffalo meat, and buffalo robes.

Without the initial help and the sharing character of the Aboriginal people, the newcomers would never have survived. Most Europeans had never hunted. English citizens in particular could not go out and kill the king's or queen's venison. Everything in the kingdom belonged to the royals, who hunted for sport and not survival. A commoner in Europe caught hunting faced severe punishment. When the newcomers got to the Americas, the Aboriginal skill and accuracy in hunting must have astounded them. Newcomers relied heavily on Aboriginal hunting skills.

The men at Fort Simpson, a fur trading post established in 1831 by the Hudson's Bay Company in Tsimshian territory near the mouth of the Nass River in British Columbia, totally depended on food provisions from Aboriginal people in that area. A notation in one of the Fort Simpson journals reads: "If the Indians don't stop celebrating soon we will starve to death." I assume it was potlatch season and the Aboriginal people were otherwise occupied with their own affairs in the business and government matters dealt with through the potlatch ceremony.

> Newcomers were trying to navigate rowboats, which were awkward, heavy, and paddled in the opposite direction.

Even though the newcomers had food all around them in the form of plants, seafood, birds, and game animals, they had no knowledge of how to get it. At Fort Alexandria on the Upper Fraser, a journal entry states: "When the Fort men ran out of food they ate their horses and, in one case, all they had left was an old bull. They killed it for food until the Indians had time to hunt or fish for them."

Aboriginal people not only supplied necessary provisions but across the continent guided newcomers on well-maintained paths used as trade routes to every part of the American continents. The only time newcomers would have had to break new trail would have been when they did not have an Aboriginal guide to lead them on well-laid out paths. Many of these paths are still used today. While I was visiting the Hudson's Bay Company Archives in Winnipeg, one of the archivists pointed out to me that many of today's major roads and highways are built on original Aboriginal trails. Of course they are! All I could do was smile and nod agreement.

Not only that, but the newcomers were trying to navigate rowboats, which were awkward, heavy, and paddled in the opposite direction. Newcomers quickly adopted the Aboriginal canoe, which was fast, light, and paddled in the same direction you are going – much easier to navigate.

ABORIGINAL PEOPLE KNEW their territory because successive generations had walked the land, named its plants, rocks, and animals, looked after it, and collectively owned it. Simon Fraser and other newcomers would never have found trails they followed to "discover" the continent without Aboriginal people showing where to find them. Nevertheless, newcomer culture believes the myth, perpetuated by popular TV shows like *Daniel Boone*, that, "When we came here this was a savage land and we tamed it with our bare hands."

Only a few Aboriginal guides are named in the history books, even though we know we played a major role in helping newcomers safely find their way. One Aboriginal guide is well-known, however: sixteen-year-old Sacagawea, who accompanied Lewis and Clark east to west from May 1804 to September 1806. Sacagawea probably used hand gestures and sign language to communicate with the diverse language groups she met along the way. Aboriginal peoples speak many different languages and so used a universal sign language to ease trade and communication between nations. In my territory, sign language was a necessary part of our culture and was used extensively during trade with other nations.

The newcomers used traditional names taught to them by the Aboriginal people for the new sights they found. Some of these names are *moose, caribou, raccoon, opossum, chipmunk, barracuda, cougar, puma, jaguar, skunk, shark, wigwam, parka, poncho, toboggan, canoe,* and *tomahawk.* Even weather descriptions such as *hurricane, chinook,* and *blizzard* come from Aboriginal languages. Place names across the Americas originated in languages of the Aboriginal people who first lived there. The traditional name for Kamloops in our nation was *Te'Kemlups* but the newcomers could not properly pronounce it and so the Anglicized version became accepted. On Vancouver Island, Nanaimo is a corruption of the name of the Snuneymuxw First Nation. In Nova Scotia, *Shubenacadie* is the Anglicized version of a Mi'kmaq word and Pictou is from the Mi'kmaq word *Piktook.* In Ontario, Mississauga is named for the nation of the Mississaugas and Toronto originated as the Mohawk phrase *tkaronto,* meaning "where there are trees standing in the water." A few other examples are *Nunavut, Yukon, Ontario, Ottawa, Manitoba, Saskatchewan, Alabama, Mississippi, Texas, Arizona, Dakota, Iowa, Nebraska,* and *Kentucky.* Heritage Canada runs an amusing Heritage Minute on TV every now and again about how Canada got its name, derived from the Iroquoian word *kanata* meaning "village." Haida Gwaii is the traditional name for the Queen Charlotte Islands and in 2010 became the official place name in recognition of a new relationship between British Columbia and the Haida people. Other nations are now using their traditional names for their territories.

IT IS ESTIMATED THAT the English language now contains about 2,200 words taken directly from the Aboriginal languages of America. The word *caucus* is an Aboriginal word and, again, did not come into the English language until the newcomers came to the Americas. The word may derive from the Algonquian *cawaassough,* meaning an advisor or someone who encourages, and was first used in Boston, Massachusetts, in the early part of the eighteenth century. Words such as *utopia* (1551), *anarchism* (1640s), *socialism* (1837), *communism* (1843), and other ideologies entered the English language only after Europeans came to the Americas.

The talking stick and the notion that only one person be allowed to speak at once with everyone respectfully listening knowing they too will get a chance to talk comes from the Aboriginal peoples. When the Europeans came to the Americas and witnessed the talking stick and the individual freedom it represents, the newcomers began to envision new forms of political life and a more egalitarian way of living. Equality and liberty as we know it today did not originate in European societies. Individual freedom in Europe was unknown because ordinary people were considered subjects of monarchical societies.

In contrast to the people who lived under European rulers, Aboriginal people did not "belong" to their leaders. The leaders in most nations did not have special privileges despite their responsibilities. Aboriginal chiefs and leaders had to earn their positions by proving their merit and accomplishments to their people. Chiefs were selected for a certain skill such as hunting, warring, or dancing. Hereditary chiefs were trained almost from birth to assume their role as leaders of their people. Since chiefs are chosen from each extended family, the system is called "hereditary." While the commonly held belief is that hereditary chiefs hold dictatorial powers, these leaders are actually subject to close control by their community and can be removed from office by them, as observed in the 1983 report of the House of Commons Special Committee on Indian Self-Government. That report also described the formalized constitution of the Iroquois, which is recited every five years by elders who have committed it to memory. The Iroquois constitution provides for a democratic system in which each extended family selects a senior female leader and a senior male leader to speak on its behalf in their respective councils. Debates on matters of common concern are held according to strict rules that allow consensus to be reached in an efficient manner, thus ensuring that the community remains unified. A code of laws, generally expressed in positive admonitions rather than negative prohibitions, governs both official and civil behaviour. Laws are passed by a bicameral legislature, made up of senior and junior houses. A council of elders oversees the general course of affairs.

The United States of America developed its constitution based on Iroquois Confederacy traditions. When the newcomer thirteen colonies were trying to put together a common government, they did not know how. These people were not royalty from their mother countries, and forming a new government was a challenge. According to American historian Bruce E. Johansen, it was Benjamin Franklin and others who studied the Aboriginal governments of the Americas and suggested a government like the Iroquois Confederacy. The end result was that the newcomers developed their own constitution based on the other. Obviously it has been changed over the years, but if you look at the U.S. Constitution and the Iroquois Confederacy, they are very similar in many ways. Bill Clinton and George Bush, when they were presidents, thanked the Iroquois for contributing to the formation of the U.S. Constitution. One has to wonder how many other countries based forms of government on that of the United States and were indirectly influenced by the Iroquois or other Aboriginal governments.

ABORIGINAL LAWS MADE sure everyone had equal opportunity and also had consequences for troublesome individuals. I am not aware of any Aboriginal tribes that had physical institutions like prisons. Traditionally members of a tribe had to conform or be banished. When there was a very serious offence, the individual was killed. Bill tells a story of his grandfather after whom he is named, Hemas Kla-Lee-Lee-Kla, dragging a man into the Big House and killing him in front of everyone. His crime? He raped a girl. Even though the perpetrator was a hereditary chief, he lost his life, and his family was banned from the community because of his action. That is how justice was dispensed at the time.

Over the years my community has banned a few people for very serious offences. During my term as chief, we were having problems with a couple of young men who were breaking and entering and otherwise being disrespectful. One was a member of our community; the other was not, but he was in a long-term relationship with someone from the community. We decided that, rather than reporting the young men to the police, we would deal with them ourselves. We informed the young men that we wanted to meet with them and that we would have to ban them unless they changed their behaviour. The young man who did not belong to our community did not want to be banned from his girlfriend's community and so came in to meet with our council and a couple of elders. His behaviour changed for the better and he eventually became a valuable member of our community.

The one who belonged to our community refused to meet with us. He said he would take his chances with the justice system. He feared being accountable to the people he had to live with in the community more than he feared legal action. These were people for whom he cared and who cared for him, but it was easier for him to go to court. He knew we could not legally ban him from the community and that he had the court system and the Department of Indian Affairs on his side. Unfortunately he has not fared so well in life. Had he not had the option of going to court he would have been forced to adjust his behaviour and probably would have also become a contributing community member.

Stories like these are common in Aboriginal communities but the newcomers in their wisdom imposed their will upon us. Now the prisons are full of Aboriginal people, each one costing the government tens of thousands of dollars. I believe that the Aboriginal way was better. Being accountable to the whole community and responsible to the people with whom you live is much more effective than being sent away and relying on a faceless justice system to provide for the cost of incarceration.

EVEN THOUGH ABORIGINAL people did not have a monopoly on freedom and individuality, they did achieve advanced cultural development of these concepts and they eventually spread to other countries. Of course giving credit where it is due is hard for those who want to believe the myth that the Aboriginal nations were waiting on the shores for someone to come and rescue them from their plight. I challenge that view with this glimpse into the contributions of Aboriginal people. My guarantee to you is that the more you research the more you will realize how much the world has adopted aspects of Aboriginal cultures. They may have been added to or altered, but without the original contribution many of the things that exist today would not exist at all or have spread around the world.

Awareness is increasing and many of the traditional ways of Aboriginal people are being embraced. Columbus did not "discover" America because millions of Aboriginal people already lived here, but the historical wisdom of the Aboriginal people is only now being explored and "discovered" by non-Aboriginals.

It grieves me to think of how much we have lost. Instead of trying to quash centuries-old civilizations, traditions, and beliefs, think how much better the world would be if we had combined all the best parts of our collective wisdom gained over the centuries. I think of the Aboriginal philosophers, historians, medicine men, healers, and all other Aboriginal leaders whose knowledge and wisdom is now diminished because of newcomer attempts to totally obliterate Aboriginal cultures. The grief is immeasurable.

WHAT IF YOUR GUESTS DECIDED TO STAY?
WOULD IT STILL BE YOUR HOUSE?

1492

Christopher Columbus voyages to the Americas

1493

Pope Alexander VI declares the Doctrine of Discovery

1763

King George III in his Royal Proclamation recognizes traditional Aboriginal land

Chapter Two

The Tilting of Power

A CLASH OF CULTURES IN THE AMERICAS

From Contact to the Early Nineteenth Century

ABORIGINAL PEOPLE HAD a culture of sharing within communities and between nations and, when the newcomers came, Aboriginal people shared with them as well. The newcomers traded steel, guns, and other goods with the Aboriginal people for fish, fur, and gold. The trade economy that resulted kept many of the Aboriginal people interested in developing and continuing a mutually beneficial relationship. Unfortunately the newcomers also brought diseases, foreign religions, and other "exchanges" that devastated the Aboriginal people.

People ask what Aboriginal communities need to do to heal. My answer is that healing has to occur on all sides and that recovery can begin only when all people are able to heal. Canadians have to abandon the deep-rooted opinion that some races are superior to others. This assumption led to the abuse of power that oppressed and displaced Aboriginal people. It is crucial for Canadians to understand the dark history of Canada and Aboriginal people. The average person needs to think about how he or she would feel and react had they been treated in a similar way.

Canada has done a good job keeping this part of its history hidden, but this is no longer possible in today's world of digital information. For some time historians have been writing about certain aspects of Aboriginal history that do not fit the accepted view of Canada. Now Aboriginal peoples are putting forward history from their perspectives. It encourages me when I go to different Aboriginal communities and hear that someone was inspired by other Aboriginal writers to start to write as well. I encourage others to keep writing even if they decide not to get published. They need to write for the benefit of our children and grandchildren. Our part in Canadian history cannot be buried with us.

IN THE EARLY years of contact Aboriginal people welcomed the newcomers as if they were new trading partners among other First Nations. Increasingly, though, interactions showed more cultural differences than similarities, particularly among basic beliefs and practices related to the use of the land, sharing of stories and history, attitude toward women, and respect for authority.

This clash of cultures was most significant in relation to views of the land and its resources. In contrast to the Aboriginal view that the land supplies you with everything you need to survive, that you take only as much as is needed, and that you share with others, the newcomers seemed to believe in "conquering" the land. Newcomer culture was to collect as much as possible for themselves and to claim parts of the land exclusively. This difference in perspectives is still the major conflict today. Now many natural resources are harvested by individuals who live in big cities and have nothing to do with the territories from which their claimed resources are extracted. Or perhaps they do live in the territory while harvesting but they then take their millions and move to the city. Destruction is left behind for those of us who live permanently in the territories. What is destroyed is the land's bounty in plant sources of food and medicine. This is the ultimate clash of cultures.

The oral culture of most Aboriginal nations was another huge difference. Newcomers have a written culture. A few Aboriginal nations like the Mayans had written records (but unfortunately the newcomers destroyed most of these records). Other nations had totem poles or ceremonial blankets that displayed their history and cultural stories. But mainly Aboriginal people had an oral culture which was used to remember a nation's history. Through oral history, each nation knows the boundaries of their territories and we are still defending them today. Then along came a culture from across the oceans bringing new devices. They had pens and pieces of paper and drew circles around huge pieces of land on maps, claiming them for monarchies such as England, France, and Spain. Maps of the Americas drawn on pieces of paper became accepted as truth in other parts of the world. The long-established territories of the Aboriginal people as recorded through oral history were ignored because they were not written on pieces of paper.

Another area of conflict related to women and our roles in Aboriginal society. Before contact, women were at least equal to men, and in matrilineal societies, women were expected to make the important decisions of the nation. The newcomer view was that women had no rights and were "chattels" of the men. In newcomer society if you "violated" a woman, compensation was paid to the father if she was not married or to the husband if she was married. The woman's rights were not considered because she was the property of a man. The newcomer culture imposed changes under the Indian Act to suit their view of women. Even some ill-advised Aboriginal men accepted the foreign notion that women are "lesser than." This has caused chaos in our Aboriginal communities. The clash of cultures between newcomers and Aboriginal people caused a shift in the balance of power as newcomers saw their own ways as superior to those of the culture they encountered in the Americas. Newcomer lack of empathy likely related to the fact that many perpetuated the inequality they had experienced in their homelands.

DESPITE WHAT WE'RE shown in the typical Hollywood movie, the first newcomers were not heroes, nobles, or knights in shining armour. For the most part, they were poor peasants fleeing oppression in their homelands. Newcomers from monarchical societies in Europe lived in poverty and servitude while the royals owned the land and had unlimited access to its resources. Wealth allowed the royals to rule over their subjects, and consequently newcomers were accustomed to being literally "lorded over." That, unfortunately, set the tone for their relationship with Aboriginal peoples. Once they were established in the Americas, instead of adopting the culture of sharing, newcomers imposed their culture of exploitation. Denied access to resources and wealth in their own countries, they found the abundant resources in the Americas irresistible.

For most newcomers, the basic reason for leaving Europe was to seek a better life and profit from resources. Fish, fur, gold, and the "saving of souls" provided the initial incentives for the explorers and new immigrants. To gain access to our resource-rich territories, newcomers relied on Aboriginal people, whose initial response was the same as with any other party in their trade networks: to share food the newcomers could not find on their own, teach them economic skills to help them adapt to wilderness life, and use their hunting and trapping skills to supply furs that the newcomers sold for huge profits in Europe. Aboriginal people regulated relationships with newcomers using the same mechanisms of ritual and ceremony that they relied on to negotiate trade networks with neighbouring tribes.

For 250 years, from the early seventeenth to the mid-nineteenth century, European demand for furs expanded trade alliances between Aboriginal people and newcomers across the Americas. Skilled Aboriginal hunters exchanged beaver pelts (used in Europe to make fashionable hats of felted beaver fur) as well as luxurious otter, fox, and wolf pelts for manufactured goods: sharp metal and woven cloth and gifts of glass beads. These were mutually beneficial exchanges that depended on co-operation between newcomers and Aboriginal people.

Many of the newcomer-Aboriginal trade alliances were articulated as treaty agreements. Often these trade alliances also included promises to assist in attacks against competing Aboriginal nations. Others were military alliances as the wars in Europe transferred to the colonies.

I HAVE HEARD many times uninformed remarks about Aboriginal rights, treaties, and Aboriginal relations with the newcomers to this land. Some people say that it was not until the hippies got involved in the 1960s and protested everything that Aboriginal people found out that they had rights. That one made me laugh out loud.

Right from the beginning Aboriginal people established their presence in traditional territories. They knew they had full sovereignty over their land and fought to protect it when needed. Today that fight still continues. But let's go back to the beginning.

At first there was no need for treaties, but as the number of newcomers increased and with so many newcomers looking for land, it became necessary to deal with the Aboriginal people in their territories.

Starting in 1701 the British Crown entered into treaties with Aboriginal people. The British made a series of peace and friendship treaties with the Mi'kmaq and Maliseet Nations between 1725 and 1779 in regions that are now New Brunswick and Nova Scotia. These treaties defined the respective rights of Aboriginal people and the British Crown's use and enjoyment of lands that Aboriginal people traditionally occupied. Treaties also promoted friendly relations between the newcomers and Aboriginal people.

The early fur trade relied heavily on the hunting and trapping skills of the Aboriginal population, and the small size of the French population of newcomers meant that land never really became an issue in competition for settlement on Aboriginal lands. Newcomers from England, however, were farmers and they first colonized territories where Aboriginals practised agriculture. In 1763, at the end of the Seven Years' War, France relinquished Canada to Great Britain and more newcomers moved in and took lands that belonged to Aboriginal peoples. With the increasing numbers of non-Aboriginal people, the relationship changed.

At about the same time, Chief Pontiac of the Odawa started to gather the nations around the Great Lakes to fight off the newcomers from encroaching on their lands. Consequently when Crazy King

George III issued a Royal Proclamation to officially claim British territory in North America after Britain won the Seven Years' War, he included in the Proclamation the foundations for dealing with Aboriginal people and their title. The Royal Proclamation explicitly stated that Aboriginal title existed and all land would be considered Aboriginal land until ceded by treaty. The Proclamation also stated that *only* the Crown could buy land from the Aboriginal nations. In turn, settlers were forbidden from buying land from the Aboriginal people and could only buy from the Crown. The Royal Proclamation recognized Aboriginal people as owning their lands and King George instructed his men to continue to sign treaties with the Aboriginal peoples. In many parts of Canada the Crown failed to do this but still illegally sold land to the settlers.

Several treaties were signed with Aboriginal people following the Royal Proclamation. These include the Upper Canada Treaties (1764 to 1862) and the Vancouver Island or Douglas Treaties (1850 to 1854). There are many disputes between the Crown and the Aboriginal people regarding the meaning of these treaties. One need only talk to any Aboriginal group that has a numbered treaty with the Crown to find out the many promises that they feel have been broken.

First Nations elders and representatives have argued for years that the written document for Treaty 9 is different than the spoken promises made during the signing. The recent discovery at Queen's University of a hundred-plus year-old diary by Daniel MacMartin, a treaty commissioner who represented the government of Ontario, supports this point of view. MacMartin's diary records oral promises that First Nations people would be able to continue to hunt throughout their territory. It does not state the contentious point that the government could take away lands for mining, forestry, or other resource development. That provision is written into the treaty document but was not negotiated with Native representatives.

Between 1871 and 1921, the Crown did enter into treaties with various First Nations, which enabled the Canadian government to actively pursue agriculture, settlement, and resource development in the Canadian North West. Because they are numbered one to eleven, the treaties are often referred to as the numbered treaties. The numbered treaties cover northern Ontario, Manitoba, Saskatchewan, Alberta, and parts of Yukon, Northwest Territories, and the northwestern part of British Columbia, but not major parts of Quebec and British Columbia, which are unceded territory, meaning that no treaties have been negotiated with the Aboriginal peoples living there. The historical treaties are the largest transfer of land from Aboriginal possession to Canada. Without these treaties Canada definitely would not be the nation that exists today.

Under these treaties, the Crown assured the Aboriginal people they would receive reserve lands, farm equipment, animals, annual payments, ammunition, clothing, and certain rights to hunt and fish. The Crown also promised to maintain

Between 67.5 and 106.4 million Aboriginal people died. You don't see that taught in the history books.

schools on reserves or provide teachers to the Aboriginal peoples named in the treaties. Treaty 6, signed in 1876 with the Cree in what is now Saskatchewan, included the promise of a medicine chest, which speaks to the unfortunate reality of Aboriginal people on the Prairies at the time. Ill health and disease brought on by contact with newcomers were a major influence in their decision to enter into the treaty. In fact, medical doctors often travelled with the treaty parties and provided medical care during negotiations.

THE NEWCOMERS CARRIED A biological catastrophe in the form of smallpox, measles, influenza, tuberculosis, bubonic plague, yellow fever, cholera, and malaria. These diseases were all unknown in the Americas before 1492 when Columbus and later explorers carrying the same diseases arrived.

It is estimated that between 75 and 95 percent of the Aboriginal people were killed by diseases brought over by the newcomers. If one accepts the estimates of how many people were in the Americas that would mean that between *67.5 and 106.4 million Aboriginal people* died. You don't see that taught in the history books.

In one of my history classes I asked the professor why Aboriginal people died in such large numbers and did not have immunity to these diseases. He didn't know the answer but said he would find out. A few days later he informed me that while Europeans had been domesticating animals and taking them out of their natural environment, the animals had developed diseases. Any penned animal will develop diseases and over time these were passed on to humans, who eventually became immune to them. Aboriginal people hunted game in nature and did not domesticate animals, aside from a few small farms in South America that raised llamas and turkeys. Thus Aboriginal people had no immunity to diseases in other areas of the world.

The diseases spread faster than the newcomers.

Aboriginal people have always said that blankets infected with smallpox were intentionally given to them by the newcomers to help rid the country of the Aboriginal presence. Anthropologist Wilson Duff traces the spread of smallpox to a newcomer with smallpox, who arrived in Victoria harbour from San Francisco in 1862. The disease quickly spread through the numerous camps of Aboriginals on the outskirts of the settlement. According to Duff: "Alarmed, the authorities burned the camps and forced the Indians to leave. They started up the coast for home, taking the disease with them, leaving the infection at every place they touched ... In the Chilcotin, a newcomer took blankets from the bodies of the dead and sold them to other Indians, who were infected in turn." Tens of thousands died.

Many Aboriginal people fled from infected areas and returned to their villages, unknowingly carrying the diseases with them and infecting those they loved the most. Historical accounts talk of the newcomers going into Aboriginal villages and finding absolutely no one there.

If your city, town, or village today lost 75 to 95 percent of the population, lost would be your leaders, artists, teachers, holy men and women, warriors, healers, and your elders who carry the knowledge. This would have a devastating effect on those few remaining. In their wake, the diseases left emotionally depressed and socially incapacitated people. The diseases had a huge impact culturally, because the majority of Aboriginal people passed on their history through oral instruction. In most cases, there would have been few records to preserve and help rebuild detailed aspects of their history, culture, and belief system.

The millions of dying Aboriginal people made room for the newcomers and allowed them to shape the land and laws to their advantage. This made it easier to dispossess Aboriginal people of their traditional lands. That did not mean that Aboriginal people accepted what was happening to them. From first contact to today, Aboriginal people have not given up their fight to have their legitimate title and rights recognized.

STARVATION WAS ALSO a factor in the dominance of newcomer culture. James Daschuk, a professor of kinesiology and health studies at the University of Regina, used medical records, socio-economic data, and analysis of environmental conditions and public attitudes to document starvation across the Canadian prairie in the 1800s, at the time Sir John A. Macdonald envisioned a railway from sea to sea as a way to link one nation, Canada.

By Confederation in 1867 the Aboriginal people who survived disease were seen as impediments to progress. The national dream of Sir John A. Macdonald required clearing the Prairies of Aboriginal people to make way for a railway and settlements from coast to coast. Daschuk documents ways in which Macdonald, acting as both prime minister and minister of Indian affairs, denied rations so as to force the Aboriginal population to relocate to reserves away from the Canadian Pacific Railway. Daschuk found the directives Macdonald sent to federal officials telling them to deny food to the First Nations. He found public statements in which Macdonald boasted about keeping the Aboriginal population "on the verge of actual starvation" to save government funds. Daschuk's conclusion: "The uncomfortable truth is that modern Canada is founded upon ethnic cleansing and genocide."

Less than a decade after Confederation, the most oppressive and racist legislation in Canada, the Indian Act, was put in place. It was not the intention of government or any federal legislation to assist the Aboriginal people. The assumption was that Aboriginal people were inferior and would simply die or be absorbed into the dominant society.

What newcomers exchanged for the land and wealth taken was starvation of the Aboriginal people who had helped them survive harsh winters and shared their wealth to feed and house them.

WHAT IF YOU WOKE UP ONE MORNING
AND FOUND YOUR FAMILY HAD DIED?
WOULD IT BE RIGHT FOR THE
NEWCOMERS TO OCCUPY THE HOUSE
LEFT EMPTY BY THOSE DEATHS?

1808

Secwepemc Chief Logshom guides explorer
Simon Fraser

1859

Tomaah leads newcomers to gold in the
Cariboo region

1862

Smallpox kills one third of Aboriginal
population in Canada

Chapter Three

Case Study in Colonial Contact

HISTORY OF THE XAT'SÚLL COMMUNITY

Early Nineteenth Century to 1876

THE HISTORY OF OUR COMMUNITY, the Xat'súll First Nation, is representative of the colonial experience of Aboriginal people in Canada. Along with other members of the Secwepemc Nation, our people occupy the largest land base within the interior of what is now British Columbia. At one point we had thirty-two campfires (communities) but now only seventeen remain. My community, Xat'súll, is the northernmost community of the Secwepemc Nation and one of the smallest. We have a few more than four hundred members. Our reserve is situated just north of Williams Lake, British Columbia.

My grandfather, Walter Sam (I called him *Xp'e7e*, which sounds like "Ba-ah") and grandmother, Sarah Sam (née Baptiste), lived in traditional ways and showed me how to gather food from the land. I travelled with my grandparents during the summer months until the age of twelve, when my grandfather died. I continued to learn from my grandmother.

When I was growing up all the kids learned how to forage and gather by going out with their relatives and being around the process. Younger kids learned which berries were good to eat and which ones to stay away from. I remember a story told to me by a non-Aboriginal woman who went picking *sxúsem* (soapberries) with a group of Aboriginal women. She had become detached from the group because usually berry pickers spread out over an area so everyone has a few berry bushes of their own from which to fill their buckets. This non-Aboriginal woman was picking berries alone, slowly filling her bucket one berry at a time; when the group came back together again, she couldn't understand how the Aboriginal women had filled their buckets so quickly yet she had so few. The children in the Aboriginal community would have found it amusing to see her picking *sxúsem* one by one. What you do is lay something like a mat or blanket under the *sxúsem* bush and then hit the branches with a stick. The ripe berries fall off easily and you then scoop them up and put them in your bucket before moving on to the next bush. Unless you grew up doing this, you would not know the different ways to pick berries.

Fish-processing techniques were taught by doing. My daughter, Jacinda, had brought some fish up from Bella Coola a few years ago. My granddaughters, Mya and Kiara, were about four and five years old at the time. Jacinda's son, Orden, was older and pretty much a pro by this time, and he was helping with the cleaning and cutting of the fish. The girls' job was to take the fish that were stored in the big tub of water and bring them to the adults at the table who would clean them. Some of the fish were quite heavy, and in order to manoeuvre without dropping them, the girls had to hold the fish close to their bodies, resulting in their clothes reeking with fishy smells; nevertheless, they took pride in doing their important job. The girls then had to take the cleaned fish and put them in a different tub of clean water. I remember at one point taking a break from cleaning the fish and watching what they were doing. Anyone who has ever cleaned fish knows that yellow jackets come from miles around to feast on the fish being cleaned. The yellow jackets don't bother us; very rarely does anyone get stung, and so no one pays much attention to them. If there are too many yellow jackets on the fish you are cutting you can brush them off with the knife. Mostly the yellow jackets go for the fish guts, where they can gorge themselves. The vision that sticks in my mind is these two girls taking their job so seriously and making sure they were not going too slow. In their haste they had hundreds of yellow jackets flying around them but they paid no attention to a scene that would terrify other children that age. They were proud of the work they were doing and we were all proud of them for doing their part in preparing for the winter.

I carried on much of what I learned until my kids were grown and on their own. Now the younger generation is learning to take over. Unfortunately not everyone in the community upholds these traditions because you have to go long distances now and not everyone has a car. In our community elders and those who know now take younger children and adults out and show them how to do things that are not practised routinely anymore, things like harvesting birch bark, cedar, spruce roots, and medicines. These practices are now limited because of resource extraction, water pollution, and "private property" that denies access.

THE XAT'SÚLL FIRST NATION is a member of the Secwepemc, the largest tribal group in the interior of British Columbia. Secwepemculecw (the traditional territory of our Secwepemc people), stretches from the Bowron Lakes in the north, east to the Columbia River Valley, south to the Arrow Lakes and beyond, and west to the Chilcotin Plateau.

Xat'súll is a Secwepemctsin (the language of the Secwepemc people) word with no literal English translation. It conveys the idea of being "on the edge," reflecting the fact that the Xat'súll village is located on a bench at the edge of the Fraser River.

Slightly more than half of the members of the Xat'súll First Nation live on one of the two reserves. Others live in Vancouver, the Fraser Valley, Kamloops, Prince George, Williams Lake, and elsewhere in the province and around the world.

In Secwepemctsin, *Kekewes e Muts* means "those who are away from home." Although many Xat'súll members choose to live elsewhere for personal, economic, or educational reasons, they remain part of our community and our traditional territory.

FOR CENTURIES, THE people of Xat'súll hunted, fished, and gathered from the land, practising an economy based on subsistence and stewardship. Stewardship means we cared for the land and its resources to ensure healthy ecosystems sustained in the long term and maintained through the body of knowledge about nature gained while subsisting on the land. To us, subsistence and stewardship also mean living as part of the natural world. In fact, the word for our territory, *Secwepemculecw*, joins land, water, and people as one.

> To us, subsistence and stewardship also mean living as part of the natural world. In fact, the word for our territory, *Secwepemculucw*, joins land, water, and people as one.

Contrary to some modern views, a subsistence economy is not simple. Rather, it is a complex system that demands organized labour from practically every man, woman, and child in a community and a deep understanding of the patterns and cycles of nature.

Nor was the social structure of our ancestors a simple one. They operated the community according to a complex code of participation, partnership, and obligation. They had unwritten codes of customs and behaviour that ensured a strong spiritual relationship among humans, plants, and animals. Government was by hereditary chief, who had responsibility for the well-being of all community members. In response, it was expected that everyone would share, and if you did not, that was breaking the Secwepemc law and you would be dealt with accordingly.

In the Secwepemc language, as in many other Aboriginal languages, there is no word for "please." Xat'súll elder Cecilia DeRose, a fluent Secwepemctsin speaker, told me there is no word for *please* because Aboriginal people did not have to beg to get what they needed. The culture of sharing provided what each community member needed to get by.

NATURE ALSO PROVIDED. Sockeye and spring salmon were plentiful in the Fraser River, and our ancestors built some of their settlements above the fishing sites we still use today. Using dip nets made from juniper and spruce saplings, willow bark, and other materials, they caught enough fish not only to feed the entire community during the summer, but also to smoke and dry for use throughout the winter and to trade and barter with neighbouring First Nations and others. We continue the practice of fishing at these ancient fishing sites today.

Our ancestors also harvested freshwater fish such as trout, kokanee, and suckers from lakes as nearby as Tyee Lake, Blue Lake, and Forest Lake and as distant as Big Lake, Mud Lake, Quesnel Lake, Horsefly Lake, Ghost Lake, and Bosk Lake.

The meat of game animals such as deer, rabbit, grouse, muskrat, bear, and beaver and birds such as ducks and geese was, and in many cases still is, another important part of the traditional Xat'súll diet. Game is generally available year round. The hides of deer and fur-bearing animals are also very useful for clothing.

Plants were the third main staple of our ancestors' diet. They travelled, as we do today, throughout our territory in search of berries, roots, bulbs, and tubers. Saskatoon berries (*speqpeq7úwi*), huckleberries (*wenéx*), strawberries (*ketqítq'e*), and soapberries (*sxúsem*) were among the most popular berries. The mountain potato (*skwenkwínem*) was another favourite.

Plants also served purposes other than food. Pitch and other plant products were used as medicine. Birch bark was used to build baskets and canoes. The rainforest around Quesnel Lake was especially important for cedar and spruce, as well as for medicinal plants that we cannot get in any other part of our territory.

Although salmon could be harvested without straying far from the current Xat'súll village, game and plants were a different matter. When the salmon weren't running, our ancestors spread throughout our traditional territory in pursuit of their subsistence economy. One of their most ingenious inventions was the *C7ístkten'* or pit house, an underground pit dwelling that distinguished the Northern Secwepemc from their Carrier and Chilcotin neighbours, who generally used simpler and more temporary above-ground shelter. In fact, Alexander Mackenzie reports that the Carrier made fun of the Secwepemc for living underground.

Our ancestors did not live in isolation from their Aboriginal neighbours. In fact, the evidence shows that they were great traders long before the arrival of Europeans. Examples of obsidian, greenstone, and the ocean shells known as dentalium have been located in Northern Secwepemc archaeological sites, evidence of a trade route from the Pacific to the Rocky Mountains. Our ancestors also conducted a lively trade of salmon with the Chilcotin and some Carrier but now mobility allows all tribes to harvest their own.

OUR ANCESTORS TRAVELLED widely over our traditional territory as we followed the seasons. Some of the more important areas in our traditional stories include the Fraser River between Marguerite and Williams Creek, Quesnel Lake at Likely but also the South Arm, Cariboo Lakes, including Cariboo Island, Horsefly, Buckskin, Tyee, Spanish, Ghost, and Forest Lakes, Bull Mountain and Big Camp. Many of these locations have remains of substantial Secwepemc settlements. All are still used by Xat'súll families today.

Our lives also followed the seasons. In the cold winter months we told stories, providing the younger generations with an understanding of our history, culture, and our relationship to the land. In the spring, the earth came out of hibernation and life began again. Spawning lake trout were available at a number of lakes but most of the Xat'súll went to Tyee Lake. The traditional name *yucwt* means to flow downstream into a river or creek. Spring also was the time to collect roots and birch to make new baskets.

As spring gave way to summer, other roots that the Xat'súll people depended on became numerous, but mostly it was a time to prepare for the salmon runs. When the first spring salmon was caught, it was a feast, a celebration, the return of life. Very soon after came the sockeye. Meanwhile the many berries were everywhere for the gathering. The season for reaping the harvest had begun. Drying racks and life along the river came alive once again.

The months of August and September, when the deer and moose are fat, was the time for hunters to test their skills and accuracy. Hunting of caribou took place in the Cariboo Mountains. Families spread out, preferring different areas such as Quesnel Forks, Horsefly, Likely, and Forest Lake.

Our ancestors were completely self-sufficient in their territories, with the land providing everything they needed. After the newcomers came, our ancestors acquired European products. But the truth is that they had them before they actually met Europeans. Our ancestors had iron bars and other European materials when Alexander Mackenzie, probably our first European contact, arrived in 1793 and trade with newcomers was established. We have seen how for many years European traders were utterly dependent on the Secwepemc and Carrier for their survival.

WHEN BRITISH COLUMBIA CELEBRATED its 150th birthday in 2008 there was great emphasis put on the fact that Simon Fraser travelled the Fraser River by canoe. He was the first non-Aboriginal to explore the area down the Big River that the Secwepemc call *Setekwe* but that is now named the Fraser, taking the name of this newcomer explorer. What was not emphasized again is the fact that had it not been for Aboriginal guides, Aboriginal food supplies, Aboriginal transportation methods, Aboriginal medicines, and Aboriginal technology to mend canoes, Simon Fraser probably would have never achieved his goal. It is well established in our oral history that Logshom, the chief of my community, guided Simon Fraser more than three hundred kilometres through Secwepemc territory and turned him over to the Stl'atl'imx (Lillooet) people to guide him farther.

All along the way, Logshom helped Fraser, his sixteen voyageurs, and two clerks navigate rapids and immense eddies formed as the massive Upper Fraser passes through vertical rock faces and steep canyon walls. Fraser never names this chief, his guide, who in addition to providing supplies of dried salmon, roots, and oil, helped smooth the way for these newcomers by acting as ambassador with First Nations along the way. The Xat'súll chief was not named until a century later, when James Teit, a Scottish anthropologist who lived among the Nlaka'pamux, interviewed Secwepemc people who had witnessed Fraser and his party come down the Fraser River with canoes. "They depict a situation of warm exchange. Neither afraid nor hostile, [they] shared their food supplies liberally, smoked, and welcomed the newcomers with pomp and ceremony," writes historian Wendy Wickwire in her exploration of contact narratives.

> Without the consent of our ancestors or regard for our Aboriginal title, Britain asserted "sovereignty" and claimed "underlying title" to the traditional territory of Xat'súll.

Fraser refers to Logshom only as "The Chief," extending some respect for his and his people's kindness. Without Logshom's advice to avoid dangerous rapids such as those west of what is now Williams Lake and to cut trails into the steep bank for portage, Fraser's party would surely have drowned. As they had earlier for Alexander Mackenzie navigating the Peace River to the sea (1792–1793), and later David Thompson on the Columbia River (1811), First Nations welcomed and guided Simon Fraser and his men.

The fur trade produced the first significant external impact on the social, cultural, and economic structure of the Xat'súll. Over time, the people of Xat'súll became directly involved in the fur trade. Power shifted from traditional leadership to the newcomers, who became wealthy through the fur trade. European diseases began their devastating impact on our people. As we know, these diseases spread faster than European settlement so, by the time Europeans arrived in Secwepemc territory in the middle of the nineteenth century, many of our ancestors were already dead.

Even though the fur trade brought numerous social problems to Xat'súll, it was generally marked by mutual respect between First Nations and newcomers. Settler numbers were small and there was no real attempt to take over ownership of our territory.

By 1846, however, the British were in renewed conflict with the United States of America over the settlement and development of western North America. To settle the dispute, Britain and the U.S. signed the Oregon Treaty of 1846, establishing the 49th parallel as the general boundary between lands held by the United States (to the south) and Britain (to the north).

In signing this agreement, without the consent of our ancestors or regard for our Aboriginal title, Britain asserted "sovereignty" and claimed "underlying title" to all Aboriginal territories, including the traditional territory of Xat'súll.

GOLD WAS DISCOVERED in the lower Fraser Canyon in 1858, which led to a huge influx of gold miners, many of whom came from the recently depleted gold fields of California. These miners travelled farther and farther up the Fraser in pursuit of gold. In 1862, led by Secwepemc and Carrier guides, Europeans struck gold in the Cariboo, the richest strike being in the area now known as Barkerville. A Secwepemc named Tomaah had led prospectors to discover gold at Horsefly in June 1859, earlier than the Barkerville claim in 1861. According to Alex P. McInnes, son of J.P. McInnes, the first gold commissioner of the Cariboo, it was a Secwepemc who took prospector Peter Dunlevey and a party of four other men to the big strike at Horsefly.

Thousands of miners came into Xat'súll territory. The town of Soda Creek was established just a couple of kilometres north of Xat'súll and immediately became a boom town. Located at the first part of the Fraser River north of Yale navigable by steamboat, it was the final stop on the stagecoach route that came through Deep Creek from Ashcroft, and the start of the boat journey that took people north on the Fraser River.

With the influx of Europeans, diseases became epidemic in Secwepemc communities. Whole villages were wiped out, including Beaver Valley, Big Lake, Quesnel Lake, and Buckskin, just across the river from Xat'súll. The survivors of Buckskin moved to Xat'súll and are among our ancestors. Gold-mining activities polluted rivers and spawning streams, killing off many of the previously abundant salmon and devastating this important food source for our ancestors. As time went by, more and more of our surviving ancestors supplemented fishing, hunting, and gathering with wages earned as miners or packers.

BY 1865, THE CARIBOO Gold Rush was dying down, but the region was now open for settlement by farmers, ranchers, and others. To ensure that most of the land was available to these newcomers and still set aside some land for our ancestors, the colonial government of British Columbia created "Indian reserves." The job of establishing Indian reserves in the Interior was left to the colony's gold commissioners. The gold commissioner for the Cariboo between 1863 and 1864 was William Cox. The chief commissioner of lands and works at the time, Joseph Trutch, delegated Cox to set aside reserve lands for our community. Unfortunately, Cox kept poor records and lost others. As a result, even though it was commonly thought that a reserve had been created for our ancestors at Xat'súll during this period, there were no written records of it. Earlier, another reserve location had been planned. Governor James Douglas signed treaties in 1850–1854 on Vancouver Island, but also, as chief commissioner, had travelled to my community, telling Koe-mu-salz, the chief at the time, to mark off the boundaries of land the band wanted to protect. Even though we travelled our territory extensively to hunt, fish for lake trout, and gather medicines, berries, and other plants, the chief of Xat'súll at the time marked out land twenty miles by seven miles to ensure protection of the land and salmon fishing places of my people. If Douglas had remained chief commissioner that probably would have become our reserve, but Douglas retired in 1864, leaving Joseph Trutch in charge of Aboriginal lands policy. Trutch took a different approach than had Douglas and denied the existence of Aboriginal land title. Trutch defined our reserve as a piece of land one

The job of establishing Indian reserves in the Interior was left to the colony's gold commissioners.

mile square and situated on a hillside that no one else wanted. Our ancestors at Xat'súll objected, saying that that piece of land was going to slip into the Fraser River. It took more than a hundred years for their prediction to come true, but in the early 1990s a big part of the reserve was lost in a landslide. Over the years, Tom Sellars, a former chief, had teased one of our elders about her house being the first that would slip into the river. I didn't understand at the time and asked what he meant. He told me the oral history of our community and the location. I thought it unlikely at the time but twenty years later our main village at Soda Creek had to be relocated because the hillside started to slide. Few people live there now. Our ancestors knew the land intimately and likely knew that underground streams would eventually cause the ground to give way.

It wasn't until 1881 that Peter O'Reilly, the Indian commissioner, confirmed "the old reserve" of 1,125 acres at the mouth of Soda Creek. However, he was concerned that our chief at the time, Koe-mu-salz, would not agree. O'Reilly wrote: "I am most anxious that the reserve question should be settled with the Soda Creek Chief for he is the most influential of all the chiefs in this section, and at the same time, the most desperate when excited by passion. All the Indians fear him, and would not dare to resist his orders."

When they met on June 10, 1881, Koe-mu-salz told O'Reilly that he had been waiting for five years for a meeting, and was sorry that the Queen had sold Xat'súll's land. According to O'Reilly: "He then stated that he wanted for his people the tract of land extending from the mouth Williams Lake Creek to seven miles above the steamboat landing, a distance of about twenty-two miles, and extending back from the river seven miles, including the farms of Messrs. Hawks, Collins, Dunlevy, and Pinchbeck, and also the town of Soda Creek."

O'Reilly described this demand as "unreasonable." Accordingly, he and Koe-mu-salz were never able to agree. On May 16, 1891, three reserves were approved for the people of Xat'súll – one at Xat'súll itself, one about ten kilometres south at Whiskey Creek, and one at Deep Creek. Xat'súll and Whiskey Creek were described as "long established settlements ... improved by the Indians."

It was later claimed by a surveyor named Fletcher that the Whiskey Creek site had been abandoned and that the Indians "did not want it." O'Reilly apparently accepted this unreliable evidence and deleted the Whiskey Creek Reserve.

It could be that this piece of land was where a newcomer wanted to settle, as illustrated by another piece of our property. There is a little piece of land labelled Lot 49 on the Soda Creek Indian Band Reserve #1. Part of the one-mile squared was a beautiful piece of property that sits on the banks of the Fraser River. A newcomer wanted to build a flour mill there. Our ancestors said no because we didn't have enough land for our families. The newcomer went to the Department of Indian Affairs and got permission to build his business on this beautiful spot over the Fraser River. Even though our people did not want him there, they had no say in the matter.

The chief of our neighbouring community of T'exelcemc, the Williams Lake Band, wrote long letters voicing inequities of land grants in our territories. One letter was published in the Victoria *Times Colonist* in 1879. In part, Chief Willy'am's letter states:

> The land on which my people lived for five hundred years was taken by a white man.
>
> He has crops of wheat and herds of cattle. We have nothing, not an acre.
>
> Another white man has enclosed the graves in which the bones of our fathers rest and we may live to see their bodies turned over by his plough.
>
> Any white man can take three hundred and twenty acres of our land and the Indians cannot touch an acre.
>
> Her Majesty sent me a coat, two ploughs, and some turnip seed.
>
> The coat will not keep away the hunger, the ploughs are idle, and the seed is useless because we have no land.

Chief Willy'am closes his letter stating: "Land, land, a little of our own land, that is all we ask from her Majesty. / If we had the deer and the salmon we could live by hunting and fishing." For this Secwepemc chief, as for the majority of Aboriginal leaders, the solution lay in the land and access to it.

OUR ANCESTORS WERE removed from the land in many ways, but one of the most debilitating was through the introduction of Christianity and the containment of children in residential schools. Our ancestors were first exposed to Christianity through French voyageurs and fur traders, many of whom partnered with and learned from Secwepemc women. So by the time missionaries first came to the Xat'súll territory in 1842 with the Catholic order known as the Oblates of Mary Immaculate, they were already somewhat familiar with this new faith.

Through the establishment of the Saint Joseph's Mission in 1867 near the Sugar Cane Reserve, the Oblates attempted to convert the Northern Secwepemc communities to the Catholic faith, to change their lifestyles, and to encourage them to use log cabins, raise livestock, and practise a European style of agriculture. The Oblates sought to eliminate traditional social structures and cultural beliefs and replace them with Christian European ones.

A "Christian" education was felt by the Oblates to be a necessary step in achieving this change. As a result, several generations of Xat'súll children and youth were forcibly removed from their families, traditional communities, and lifestyle and indoctrinated into non-Native customs, education, and ethics. Children were separated from their families and traditional teachings. They were forbidden to speak Secwepemctsin. Over the years, the Mission school became more like a prison, with widespread physical, sexual, and emotional abuse, as related in my book *They Called Me Number One*, which shares the experience of three generations of my family who attended residential school.

Coupled with the loss of our people through disease and the loss of our lands through European settlement, this alienation and abuse of our young people led to a sharp decline in the health of our community from the late nineteenth century, well into the twentieth century.

WHAT IF THE NEWCOMERS BEGAN TO FILL
THE HOUSE AND OUTNUMBER YOUR FAMILY?
DOES THAT MAKE THE HOUSE THEIRS?

1876

Indian Act legislated

1884

Potlatch, sundance, and other traditional
government practices banned

1910

Chiefs meet with Prime Minister Wilfrid Laurier

Chapter Four

Workarounds
and Memorials

EARLY EFFECTS OF THE INDIAN ACT

1876 to 1920s

WHEN I WAS elected chief in 1987 I was fully aware that the Indian Act existed and that it was supposedly legislation for on-reserve lands and people – but I refused to read it. When Department of Indian Affairs officials would come out to our community wanting to dictate this or that, for the most part I ignored their "advice" unless we needed to follow procedure to gain monies. I did not read any parts of the Indian Act until I went to law school in 1998. As I suspected, that piece of racist legislation only enraged me. Leaders before me in all parts of Canada felt the same way.

The Indian Act caused chaos in the lives and cultures of Aboriginal people. Despite all the assistance Aboriginal people had provided the newcomers, despite all the Aboriginal contributions to the rest of the world, despite any intelligence shown by any individual, through the paternalistic Indian Act, "Indians" were put into the same category as children and the mentally disabled. The average Canadian would not have tolerated the laws that were applied to Indians.

Once the Indian Act was legislated, we Aboriginal people did not throw up our hands and say, "Well, that's the law. We have to obey it." Aboriginal people were constantly trying to get around or disregard the racist legislation and many spent time in jail for not accepting "the law."

During my terms as chief we had many community meetings but nowhere under the Indian Act does it require that chiefs and councils do anything for their community members. The only obligations we have are to the Department of Indian Affairs and other funders. We held community meetings out of a sense of obligation to communication between leader and community that is traditional to Aboriginal culture. We worked around the Indian Act, as generations of Aboriginal people have done since it was first established.

WHEN THE INDIAN Act was enacted in 1876, it was instituted without any input from Aboriginal people. The Canadian government did not ask Aboriginal people what they thought of the new legislation that would govern their lives. The government simply wrote the law and imposed it on us.

Through this racist legislation, newcomers gave themselves the power and the authority to make decisions over Aboriginal people from the time we are born until we die – even after death in the administration of the estate of an Aboriginal person. The Indian Act created an authoritative institution – the Department of Indian Affairs – that wielded political control over Aboriginal people. The act also imposed government structures in the form of band councils, established limited access to the land through the reserve system, and defined who qualifies as Indian.

Each time the government realized its laws were not working, they amended the act. Repeated amendments have been made to deal with unanticipated problems that arose while trying to "civilize and assimilate" the Indians, the overall purpose of the act.

IT WAS THE British North America Act, 1867, that initiated the transfer of responsibility for Canada's Aboriginal people under the Proclamation of 1763 from the British Crown to the colony. Then, in 1869, despite the Aboriginal people having their own government structures that had worked for them, the Department of Indian Affairs imposed the elected band council system. An Act for the Gradual Enfranchisement of Indians, 1869, imposed European-style elections, undermining the traditional structure of governance by hereditary chiefs. The 1876 Indian Act reinforced the elected band system. In response, the Aboriginal people simply elected their traditional or hereditary chiefs. To stop this, the department went back and in 1884 changed the Indian Act so that they could annul the election of any chief found guilty of "fraud or gross irregularity." The chief could be charged with a "sham election." Once convicted, the chief could not run for another position in a band election for six years. This amendment, in effect, marked the beginning of an overt attack on the traditional government system of Aboriginal people in Canada.

> Women had traditionally been leaders among Aboriginal people but under newcomer legislation, they had status only through marriage to men.

In addition, only Indian men were allowed to vote in band elections. This effectively removed Indian women from band political life. For matrilineal cultures this was devastating. Women had traditionally been leaders among Aboriginal people but under newcomer legislation, they had status only through marriage to men.

A FURTHER UNDERMINING OF ABORIGINAL power was the Indian Act definition of who qualified as "status Indians." The Indian Act of 1876 did not take into account the differences between Aboriginal nations. In British Columbia, for example, the Coastal nations are much different than those from the Interior. Across Canada Aboriginal nations were as culturally different as the European people consider themselves to be, but none of that was conceived of.

The French would not consider themselves the same as the Irish nor would the British consider themselves to be the same as the Spanish. Yet even though the situation was the same, Aboriginal nations were viewed as one ethnicity, one homogeneous culture, one faceless group, and all became "Indian" under the Indian Act.

The Department of Indian Affairs took it upon itself to decide who was and was not an "Indian." Beginning in 1850, the colonial government compiled lists of Indians and the names of members of each Indian band. These lists became the "Indian Register," the official record of all those eligible for "rights and benefits" as status Indians in Canada. No person could be added to the list without official approval from the Indian agent, the government representative who administered Indian affairs at the regional level. Those who wanted to be included on the list with their families but were away hunting or fishing when the list was compiled were sometimes omitted.

This fact is common knowledge in most areas of Canada. We have status and non-status in every region. We know that when the lists were being prepared people were away fishing, hunting, trapping, or whatever. Many of the ones who were left off the Indian status lists have been added only since Bill C-31 came into effect in 1985. Our community had many members added. This has created tensions within Indian bands and economic hardship because the membership increased but the money to accommodate the new members did not.

Meanwhile there were many officially considered Indian who did not want to be on the Indian Register. They did not want to be subjected to the oppressive laws. Removal of a name from the register was called "enfranchisement" and meant an Aboriginal person was no longer considered an Indian. Enfranchisement meant you no longer needed permission for every aspect of your life. Aboriginal people considered enfranchisement a matter of personal choice and self-determination; newcomers considered enfranchisement a privilege. Only Indian men could seek enfranchisement but a man's wife and children would automatically be enfranchised with him regardless of their wishes. To be enfranchised the man had to be over age twenty-one, able to read and write either French or English, be reasonably well educated, free of debt, and of good moral character as determined by a commission of non-Aboriginal examiners. There was no appeal procedure if an Indian was turned down for enfranchisement.

There was also no appeal if the Department of Indian Affairs determined an Indian should lose their status. Becoming a status Indian did not mean you could stay Indian forever. The Department of Indian Affairs in their infinite wisdom determined that Indians who went beyond residential-school education, who might want to earn a university degree or become clergymen, were automatically enfranchised. This thereby barred any persons with formal education from entering reserve lands; once you were enfranchised you could be charged with trespassing – even if all your family lived there.

ABORIGINAL PEOPLE WERE also undermined by restrictions on where we could live. Historically Aboriginal people always picked the best places to build their communities. Who wouldn't?

At one time we had all of our territories to service the needs of all our people and sharing was a required part of our culture. The resources were harvested on a rotational basis to keep the land healthy. We moved around within our territories to manage the resources and to avoid overharvesting in some areas. When the newcomers came and the power tilted their way, they realized that those were the pieces of land they wanted, and they took them.

Reserve lands were established under many of the treaties signed after the Proclamation of 1763. When the Indian Act of 1876 was enacted, it restricted reserve size and dictated the ways in which reserves would be governed by the federal government. Many letters were written by Aboriginal leaders across Canada protesting the small amount of land; our leaders at Soda Creek did the same.

Once we were placed onto reserves it was pretty well each family for themselves in order to survive. Small pieces of reserve land that were expected to supply all our needs created a lot of problems for our people. Families ended up fighting with each other for what few resources could be accessed. That is one reason why families within almost every Aboriginal community are so split. We have only small pieces of land to grow gardens or raise a few cattle or horses. The one-mile square that our community was allowed was not enough for all the families living there. The small piece of land had to supply everyone with everything they needed to survive. Even today the land is still not adequate.

TRADITIONAL LAND-HOLDING PRACTICES were further straitjacketed by amendments to the Indian Act. In 1894 Indian bands lost the power to decide whether non-Aboriginals could reside on or use reserve lands. After that date the Department of Indian Affairs was the sole authority for determining who could or could not live on reserve land. In addition, great pressure was put on many bands to surrender portions of their reserves so they could be sold to settlers or annexed to municipalities. Originally Aboriginal people had lived where all the towns and villages of Canada exist now. As the towns grew bigger, newcomers needed more land and Aboriginal people were moved completely away from their original villages. For example, the Songhees First Nation had a huge village on lands where the Parliament Buildings now stand in Victoria, the capital city of British Columbia. In the 1990s the Songhees sued the federal government on the basis of historical amendments to the Indian Act and in 2006 accepted a settlement of $31.5 million for the wrongful expropriation of lands.

> The one-mile square that our community was allowed was not enough for all the families living there.

Even though many of the Indian reserves were in places the newcomers did not initially want, sometimes those pieces of land later became valuable. Frank Oliver, who was appointed Minister of the Interior in 1905, stated in the House of Commons in 1906: "If it becomes a question between Indians and the whites, the interests of the whites will have to be provided for."

In 1911, an amendment to the Indian Act allowed a judge to issue a court order to move a reserve that was within or adjoining a town. The judge's order was issued without band consent or surrender before the entire community was moved. This provision was considered necessary so that Parliament could avoid the tedious and months- or even years-long task of passing special legislation every time it wished to expropriate reserves adjoining towns. The court order sped up the process immensely. If you take a close look across Canada you will see many examples of special legislation such as this; in fact, my neighbouring Secwepemc community, the Williams Lake Indian Band, is a perfect example.

Unfortunately Frank Oliver's statement about newcomers having first priority still rings true today and that is evident in the treaty negotiations around the province of British Columbia. In all our negotiations it is pretty evident that the needs of the Aboriginal people come second to any non-Native people. The government officials continually protect the interests of those who acquired the lands illegally from the province.

ANOTHER MAJOR UNDERMINING of Aboriginal authority came with amendments to the Indian Act that banned the potlatch. Many people do not understand the effect: outlawing the potlatch meant outlawing the basis of Aboriginal government. Section 3 of the amending act, signed on April 19, 1884, declared that: "Every Indian or other person who engages in or assists in celebrating the Indian festival known as the 'Potlatch' or in the Indian dance known as the 'Tamanawas' is guilty of a misdemeanor, and liable to imprisonment for a term of not more than six nor less than two months in any gaol or other place of confinement; and every Indian or person who encourages ... an Indian to get up such a festival ... shall be liable to the same punishment."

I was trying to sum up the signifigance of the potlatch ban a few years ago and had a long drawn-out explanation about why the potlatch and sundance were so important. When I explained my dilemma to Bill, he summarized it very quickly for me. He said, "Outlawing the potlatch and other forms of Aboriginal government would be similar in today's society to outlawing their parliament, outlawing their legislature, outlawing their court system, outlawing their church, outlawing their land registry office, outlawing their ministries of births, deaths, and marriages, and outlawing all other functions of their society." All these functions were carried out at a potlatch – it was more than a "festival"; it was an inter-tribal meeting and social, political, and economic exchange. Bill, and every chief before him whose name was Hemas Kla-Lee-Lee-Kla, could not, under the Indian Act, fulfill their duties as leaders once the potlatch was banned. As the front cover of this book indicates, Aboriginal leaders across Canada were caged in every way.

> Outlawing the potlatch and other forms of Aboriginal government would be similar in today's society to outlawing the newcomers' parliament, outlawing their legislature, outlawing their court system.

When the 1884 amendments prohibited the potlatch and other forms of Aboriginal gatherings, they undermined ceremonies that officiated and confirmed the social and political organization of each nation. They also undermined the oral tradition of sharing cultural information through stories and dances, performed at these feast ceremonies and witnessed by all attending the event. As part of each ceremony, witnesses were paid with gifts so that if there was a dispute later or they were called to confirm something, they had an obligation to tell the truth. Oral history and cultural instruction at work again.

Under the anti-potlatch laws ceremonial items and symbols of government were seized and in many cases never returned. There are documented cases in which those who seized them profited highly for their sale in other parts of the world. Nineteenth-century West Coast missionaries often sold off shaman rattles, ritual pipes, animal crests, and totem poles handed over to them by Aboriginal people who had converted to Christianity. Other artifacts were given to their offspring, who have made hundreds of thousands of dollars from their sale.

Also, under the anti-potlatch laws arrests were made. Bill's mom, Ethel Pearson, told the story Bill relates in his foreword to this book of how the potlatch laws were enforced by raiding a village where a big winter potlatch was taking place. It happened in the Kwakwala-Musgamagw area between the northeast tip of Vancouver Island and British Columbia's Central Coast. As Bill says, the high-ranking chiefs who had gathered were arrested and taken to jail. They had actually been framed by two individuals who received money in exchange for the information about the potlatch which had successfully gone underground for many years. The chiefs were tried in Alert Bay without legal counsel and twenty of them were shipped to Oakalla Prison Farm, where they were physically abused. Their people would paddle canoes filled with traditional food and go up the Fraser River to New Westminster and walk over the hill to the prison farm in order to feed their chiefs through the iron fence.

Chief Bill Wilson's grandfather, Hemas Kla-Lee-Lee-Kla, was one of those incarcerated. He refused to eat the food provided to him by the white jailors for fear of being poisoned, thus the canoe loads of food delivered every week. He served six months at Oakalla, living beneath a cow barn.

IN ADDITION TO THE potlatch ban, further amendments in 1895 banned traditional dances, including the Blackfoot sundance and the Cree and Saulteaux thirst dance. This ban conflicted with the desire among many newcomers to observe Aboriginal people as curiosities. One of the attractions for tourists even today are Aboriginal dances. Tourists love to go to powwows. Coastal nations today are invited to display their forms of dancing at public events in Canada and other countries. After 1895 when the newcomers wanted the Aboriginal people to "put on a show" for guests from Europe it became apparent that they needed to change the Indian Act. Instead of outlawing all cultural activities, in 1914 the Indian Act allowed Aboriginal people to participate in "Aboriginal costumes" in any "dance, show, exhibition, stampede or pageant" *but only with the official permission of the Department of Indian Affairs.*

> An Indian agent could simply tell the RCMP that such-and-such a person broke the law under the Indian Act and that person would be sent to jail.

The police were unwilling to enforce this Department of Indian Affairs policy because, if it was challenged, they felt it would be found illegal by the courts and would bring their other law enforcement efforts into question. In order to counter this, in 1918 these "offences" were brought within the Indian agent's jurisdiction thereby removing them from courts outside the reserve.

Allowing the Indian agents to "handle" these offences and removing them from the courts where everyone could be a witness to these racist laws allowed the injustices to go on unchecked. An Indian agent could simply tell the Royal Canadian Mounted Police that such-and-such a person broke the law under the Indian Act and that person would be sent to jail.

FOLLOWING RIGHT ON THE heels of hundreds of years of epidemics and dispossession of land, the residential school experience further ensured a sense of hopelessness and defeat. Beginning in the 1880s, Aboriginal children were removed from the reserves and required to attend residential schools. Children as young as four and five years old were required by Canadian law to attend these schools. These early years are the child's most vulnerable. Parents were not consulted about whether they wanted to send their children to these schools. Children suffered from emotional, physical, and sexual abuse, loss of parental guidance and family life, forced labour, loss of language and culture, neglect, denial of proper education, and inferior nutrition and health care. Children in the schools grew up in a climate of fear, apprehension, and ascribed inferiority. When these children finally left the schools, many were "time bombs" waiting to explode. Many exploded inwardly in spasms of self-hatred or self-harm, and many committed suicide. Others used drugs and alcohol to try to bury what they wanted to forget. The violence in our communities is a result of unresolved destructive behaviours stemming from their childhood experience at the schools. Anger is still too prevalent.

The quality of teaching in the schools was inferior to regular public schools. R.F. Davey, director of education services for two decades mid-century, summed it up: "Up to 1950 it was found that residential schools had been unable to attract qualified staff. Over 40 percent of the teaching staff had no professional training. Indeed, some had not even graduated from high school."

Like 150,000 other Aboriginal, Inuit, and Metis children across Canada, I was required by Canadian law at the time to attend residential school. I lived at St. Joseph's from September 1962 to June 1967. The Mission was run by the Oblates of Mary Immaculate and set in an isolated valley about sixteen kilometres south of the town of Williams Lake. The school was only forty kilometres from my home community, but it may as well have been a million. The kids from Williams Lake Indian Band were only eight kilometres from home, and yet they still did not see their families for ten months of the year.

A "half-day" system was in place until 1951, with classroom learning only for several hours. The rest of the day was labour for the children. My grandmother, who also went to St. Joseph's, remembers the school as a place of hard work. The children did everything from planting and harvesting the gardens to cutting and hauling in the hay, looking after the livestock, and anything else that required manual labour. While I was doing some research at the provincial archives in Victoria, British Columbia, I came across some letters written by the businessmen in Williams Lake. They complained about the child labour at the residential school that I attended. They complained because St. Joseph's Mission got free labour out of the children that allowed them to sell goods at lower prices, and the businesses were upset because they could not compete with these lower production costs. They wanted the government to address this unfair business practice.

The residential schools were not a place to learn social skills or to learn to think for yourself. We were more like little robots than children. "Yes, Sister. Yes, Father" was the extent of our conversations. There was no attempt to have us discuss any feeling or try to resolve whatever problems we may have had. We learned to keep whatever we were feeling deep inside. The only emotion that was safe to express was anger if we were not near any supervisors. There were many fights between students. A quote from a non-Aboriginal critic who opposed the schools said, "They learn to work under direction which doesn't require, and even discourages, any individual acting or thinking on their part." As someone who went to the schools, I can verify that is true. The experience of three generations of my family is documented in my earlier book.

Everyone in our area went to residential school unless they were sick and could not work. I was shocked to learn that Bill did not go to residential school. Some of his older brothers and one sister went to the schools but he and other younger ones did not. By the late 1940s, his mom and dad had a successful business off-reserve and refused to allow their younger children to attend the schools. I later learned that not all Aboriginal children went to the schools. Even though there were more than 130 residential schools across Canada, there would not have been enough room for all the Aboriginal children.

Some parents hid their children when the Indian agents came to gather them up for school each September. I am not sure how many were successful in keeping their children at home. At Soda Creek, St. Joseph's Residential School was so close to our reserve it was difficult to hide the children. Priests came to our community to pick up children and drive them to school at the end of each summer. Everyone was required to attend the residential school, except those who were too sick. In the 1930s my uncle Ernie was sent home because he had tuberculosis. My grandmother and her sister, Annie, nursed him better using traditional medicines.

In some Aboriginal communities, day schools were run on-reserve and the children went back to their homes at night. Alleged abuses at those schools are also emerging now.

Some Aboriginal children went to public school. Bill is eternally thankful that he did not go to the schools but he regrets the fact that he did not know until later in life the atrocities that were committed against Aboriginal children. He feels he would have been a better leader had he known. Bill's ignorance of the residential schools even allowed him to drive two nephews and a niece to the residential school in Port Alberni one September. He still beats himself up for contributing to the torture he knew nothing about.

Indian agents were the chief administrators for Indian affairs in their respective districts.

UNDER THE INDIAN ACT, money was allocated to Department of Indian Affairs offices and then the Indian agents decided how it was to be spent for the "benefit" of status Indians. The Indian agents were not responsible to the Indians and so for the most part doled it out for the benefit of compliant Indians. In 1880 an amendment to the Indian Act denied band councils the power to decide how monies from the surrender and sale of their lands or other resources would be spent.

Indian agents were the chief administrators for Indian affairs in their respective districts. The older people in my community have many stories about the local Indian agents. The Indian agent I remember from when I was a teenager in about 1969–1970 was called "Spike." He was a skinny little man with glasses and his face was never soft or had a smile on it. "You people, you people!" was the phrase I remember him saying to my mom. I did not like him at all but, of course, neither of us ever said anything to him. Most of the stories the elders have are about the ignorance of Indian agents who saw themselves as knowing what was best for Indian people. My mom said that she remembers Mr. Taylor and Mr. Christy as well. She said my grandparents hated Mr. Taylor. Over time the Indian agent became an increasingly powerful influence on band social and political matters. Mom said, "If the Indian agent called you to Williams Lake to see them, you had to go. They made us feel guilty about things even when we didn't do anything wrong. It made everyone wonder what was going on; it was not a good thing to be called to go see the Indian agent." The possibility of going to jail was always near. If the Indian agent determined that you had committed a crime or if he determined you did something wrong, then you faced consequences.

In 1882, Indian agents – along with all the other powers they had – were made "Justices of the Peace" to enforce "civilizing" regulations of the Department of Indian Affairs. They became the judge and jury for anyone labelled an Indian. Indian agents could conduct trials if they dealt with Indians. If they decided someone was guilty of an offence under the Indian Act, they simply called the Royal Canadian Mounted Police to come and arrest the person. This was a considerable extension of power for Indian agents who had no previous legal training. Of course this resulted in many dubious court proceedings and the incarceration of many of our people at Oakalla Prison Farm.

THE 1884 AMENDMENTS also made it illegal for three or more "Indians, non-treaty Indians, or halfbreeds" to gather in one place except for religious or familial purposes. The Department of Indian Affairs did not want Indians to gather and discuss issues that were important to them. This did not work for the missionaries who wanted to convert the Indians to whatever religion they were pushing. They needed to be able to get the Indians together in groups of more than three at time. And so the government went back and changed the Indian Act so that the Indians could only gather in groups of more than three for familial or religious purposes.

The Aboriginal people came up with their own ways of having their meetings. Members of the Native Brotherhood of British Columbia, one of the first and oldest organizations in the province, tell the story of gathering and singing "Onward Christian Solders" and other hymns until the Indian agent and the RCMP were sure it was a religious gathering. Once the authorities left, the Aboriginal people freely discussed the important land and human rights issues they needed to survive.

I was in the Stó:lō territory giving a presentation once, and when I was relaying this story about the "Onward Christian Soldiers," an elder laughed and told me another story about a time when the priest came for mass and asked the chief to interpret in church what the priest was saying. The chief would pretend to interpret what the priest was saying but was actually talking to the people in his language about the political issues. The elder laughed and said that this was the only way they kept the movement alive without a risk of going to jail. The human rights struggle across Canada had to go "underground" to stay alive.

In 1884 it also became an offence for "three or more Indians, non-treaty Indians or half-breeds" to "breach the peace" or to make "riotous" or "threatening demands" on a civil servant, namely the Indian agent.

By 1933, the authority of Indian agents was bolstered by a requirement that all complaints and inquiries from Aboriginal people be directed to the Indian Affairs branch *through the local Indian agent.* I wonder how many complaints were made knowing the power and possible consequences that the Indian agent had over Aboriginal lives? I would bet none.

Nations were divided up into "new" areas by the newcomers for the ease of the Indian agents and others. Communities that were too far out into the wilderness were moved closer to towns for the benefit of the Indian agents.

The Secwepemc Nation at one time was one. *Secwepemculecw* means "All the Land within the Secwepemc territory" and is approximately 180,000 square kilometres. Chiefs regularly visited other communities to keep the nation as one. The Hudson's Bay Archives document that the Kamloops chief made regular visits to Soda Creek (Xat'súll), a distance of a little more than two hundred kilometres. One of the Hudson's Bay men said, "Distance is nothing to an Indian." Over the years since the Indian Act was introduced, we have been divided and our nation and lands were assigned to three different Indian agencies: the Kootenay Agency, the Williams Lake Agency, and the Kamloops Agency. Today our tribal lands remain divided into different regional districts and other boundaries set out by the newcomers. This has prevented us from working together. Like so many other nations that have been divided, we are attempting to rebuild our Secwepemc Nation and work as one. The Northern Secwepemc have become closer to the southern Carrier and the Tsilhqot'in because of the division. I know more people in these two tribes than I do in the Southern Secwepemc communities. This situation is similar in many tribes that have been split. I was talking to a Haida person from Alaska who said he has never been to Haida Gwaii, a distance of not more than eighty kilometres by water but divided by the U.S.–Canadian border, an example of how it was that international borders also divided nations. There was no consideration at all when governments were claiming the land to try to include all of the tribal areas. For example, the Haida Nation has territorial lands in British Columbia and in Alaska. The Mohawk Nation, the Salish Nations, and other traditional tribal areas in Canada extend into the United States.

IN THE FACE of the many efforts to contain Aboriginal people, our ancestors worked to maintain access to our land and fought for the survival of our community. In 1911, Secwepemc chiefs, including Xat'súll's Chief Koe-mu-salz, joined with their fellow chiefs from the Okanagan and Thompson (Couteau) tribes, to make a declaration to then prime minister of Canada, Sir Wilfrid Laurier, about ongoing concerns. The declaration stated in part:

> We demand that our land question be settled and ask that treaties be made between the government and each of our tribes ... We desire that every matter of importance to each tribe be a subject of treaty so we may have a definite understanding with the government on all questions of moment between us and them ...

Like Aboriginal people across Canada, Secwepemc leaders have continuously tried to have their grievances dealt with. Rising political action about Aboriginal groups early in the nineteenth century resulted in the McKenna-McBride Commission, a royal commission that between 1913 and 1916 travelled around the province of British Columbia to settle the "Indian reserve question." The commission's instructions were to examine the reserves already established and to establish reserves in areas of the province where none existed. In the end, despite promises of better lands, the commission recommended the cut-off of more than 47,000 acres of valuable land and added approximately 87,000 acres of less valuable land. In Xat'súll territory this meant a significant reduction in our land base.

The Allied Tribes of British Columbia, which included Sec-wepemc Nation communities, was formed in 1915 at a meeting in Spences Bridge. Between 1916 and 1920, the Allied Tribes held protest meetings as unrest spread in Aboriginal people. By 1920 the minister of Indian affairs had introduced legislation that Parliament passed, which authorized cut-offs without the consent of Aboriginal people. The Allied Tribes retained a lawyer, and in 1926 they presented their petition to Parliament. The Tribes requested that Parliament get a legal decision from the Privy Council on the land claim, and asked for action on the social and economic problems the Aboriginal communities were facing, to no effect.

CANADA'S POLICY TO contain and assimilate our ancestors continued throughout most of the twentieth century. The potlatch and similar ceremonies were criminalized in 1884; gathering in groups or engaging lawyers to assert land claims was criminalized in 1927. These prohibitions lasted until 1951. During some periods, it was also a criminal offence to keep children out of residential schools.

As shown in this chapter, a series of Indian Act amendments and the establishment of the federal Department of Indian Affairs exerted increasing control over the people of Xat'súll and Aboriginal people across Canada.

WHAT IF EVENTUALLY YOU ARE DISPLACED
TO THE GARAGE AND THE NEWCOMERS TAKE
OVER THE REST OF THE HOUSE? IS IT THEIRS?

1924

Land removed from reserves (reserve cut-offs)
become a symbol among Aboriginal people of
newcomer deceit and immorality

1927

Aboriginal people banned from poolrooms,
dance halls, and other places of amusement
all across Canada

1939–1945

Aboriginal soldiers serve in the
Second World War

Chapter Five

Increasing Containment and Repression

AMENDMENTS TO THE INDIAN ACT

1920s to 1946

MY MOM WAS BORN in 1925, during the era when Aboriginal people were not considered citizens of Canada. Aboriginal people at this time also did not have the provincial or federal vote or the protection of Canada. Even though she was in the territory of her dad's people, my mother's human rights as a Secwepemc citizen were not considered relevant. According to newcomer Canadian law, she was considered a ward of the state of Canada and laws that resembled more of an apartheid system were imposed on her and all "Indians."

The Canadian establishment came down hard on Aboriginal people during this period. This was the most restrictive period in Canada's history and yet the Aboriginal people, by the thousands, still contributed by volunteering to defend Canada in the world wars. Even Aboriginal soldiers who went to war for Canada ended up with more problems than if they had just stayed on the reservation. Their efforts were not rewarded.

ONE MEASURE IMPLEMENTED in Canada to try to control Indians was the pass system. Introduced after the North-West Resistance in 1885, the pass system was at first to be applied only to "rebel Indians"; however, John A. Macdonald insisted that the system should be applied to all Aboriginal people. In early 1886, books of passes were issued to Indian agents, and subsequently First Nations people could not leave their reserve unless they had a pass signed by the Indian agent. The pass described when they could leave, where they could go, and when they had to return. Although the pass system was never passed into legislation and as a result was never legal, it was enforced well into the 1940s, mainly on the Prairies.

The notorious pass system was never part of the Indian Act although it was official Department of Indian Affairs policy. Indians were prosecuted if they were found off their reserves without passes. This was all within the jurisdiction of the Indian agents. And if they broke the law, the Royal Canadian Mounted Police on the command of the Indian agent arrested the Indians.

I asked my mom about whether they ever left the reserve without a pass. She said, "We knew about the pass but we didn't pay any attention to it." That was because the Williams Lake Agency included 150 Indian bands from Clinton to the Blackwater River and from Anahim Lake to the Alberta boundary. It would have been hard for one Indian agent to keep track of all the people who left the reserves and the Aboriginal people, as much as possible, ignored the racist laws.

Bill describes how ludicrous the pass system was in remote parts of British Columbia. His dad's reserve, Cape Mudge on Quadra Island, sits a few kilometres across the water from the town of Campbell River. In order to get a pass to leave the Cape Mudge reserve, an Indian had to go more than two hundred kilometres north to Alert Bay where the Indian agency was located. In other words, to legitimately get a pass an Indian would have to break the law by travelling to Alert Bay to get a pass to go just a few kilometres across the water.

The pass system was intended to prevent Aboriginal groups from collaborating with each other on political issues and participating in the banned potlatch, sundance, and other gatherings on distant reserves. It also discouraged parents from visiting their children in off-reserve residential schools. The pass system also had an economic effect on the Aboriginal peoples. It was difficult to support one's family on the small reserves and many needed to work off-reserve. The need to continually apply to the Indian agent for a pass prevented Aboriginal people from keeping jobs. Ultimately the pass system increased their economic dependency.

I found the following news tidbit from November 1937 while doing research in the Victoria Archives: "Frank Bones, Indian, was convicted of trespassing on the Canoe Creek reserve on November 1. Paid his $10.00 plus costs fine." I knew my mom knew the Bones family and I wanted to learn the story behind the article. Mom knew Frank Bones, who was from the Clinton area, but she didn't know the details of the story. It was later when I was giving a presentation to the Stswecem'c Xgat'tem First Nation in the community of Canoe Creek when an elder, Rosalie Sargent, remembered when Frank Bones was arrested. Frank was from the Clinton Indian Band and had been on his way to Canoe Creek to pick up his bride before their wedding. While there, the Indian agent caught him and charged him with trespassing on a reserve that was not his own. Frank began his married life with a hefty fine of ten dollars at a time when people worked for fifty cents a day.

In my community two women who had married non-status Indians and moved off-reserve went to visit their family on the Soda Creek reserve. Both women had been raised in the community and were related to almost everyone there. They were told by the Indian agent that they could not come onto the reserve even to visit. The reason? In marrying non-status Indians they too had lost status. As non-status Indians they could be prosecuted for trespassing.

THE PASS SYSTEM contravened international law established in the Jay Treaty, signed in 1795 between Great Britain and the United States following the American Revolution. The Jay Treaty allows Canadian Aboriginal people to pass freely across the U.S. border. Because of the Jay Treaty it is relatively easy for Canadian Aboriginal people to get U.S. Green Cards. When I was in my early teens, every year buses from the Okanagan and the United States came up and rounded up Aboriginal people to work in the orchards on both sides of the border. Every summer many of our community members, my brothers and uncles included as well as many of my young cousins, would be gone south to work in the orchards. I always envied them but my grandparents were too old and had their own work to do to prepare for the winter. Instead of crossing the border, I stayed with them.

One year, along with my older relatives, my uncle Ernie went down to the United States to work. My grandmother was surprised to see him return before the fall season had begun. It seemed that my uncle Ernie had gotten into trouble and had been serving time in Washington state for a minor offence. He escaped from jail and headed back to Canada. My grandmother was worried, thinking someone would come looking for him. She probably thought it was the same as with residential school for which they always tracked down the runaways. No law officer ever came looking for Ernie but the U.S. Sheriff sent a message through some of our relatives telling Ernie that if he ever went back to the United States he would serve a life sentence.

NOT ALL PLACES were so freely accessible by Aboriginal people. A "No Indians Allowed" policy was widely enforced across Canada. In the mid-1950s racial segregation in the Cariboo was blatant. Lenny and Cecilia DeRose, an inter-racial couple who celebrated their fiftieth wedding anniversary on December 1, 2006, talked about the challenges of being together during the first years of their marriage. (Lenny was white and Cecilia is Secwepemc.) Sage Birchwater did a story on this beautiful couple in the local Williams Lake paper *Casual Country*. "We couldn't stay in a hotel room when we were first together," said Lenny. "Indian people were not allowed in." Lenny has passed into the spirit world now but I remember asking him about it after the article came out. He still had steam coming out of his ears remembering those racist laws.

A 1927 amendment to the Indian Act gave the Department of Indian Affairs the power to regulate the operation of poolrooms, dance halls, and other places of amusement that Indians may have frequented. This amendment ensured the Indians would not spend too much time in the "leisure pursuits" that were available to non-Indians.

By 1930 a non-Indian poolroom operator could face a fine or a jail term of one month for allowing an Indian to frequent an establishment too many times. Take note that the restriction was placed on the poolroom operators because there was constant resistance from the Aboriginal people and the Indian agents could not be everywhere at the same time. The significance is that once legislators decided poolroom operators would be fined, it allowed any poolroom operator to legally ban all Indians. This did the job for the Indian agent; he did not continually have to make sure the Indians were not frequenting certain places. The owners did not want to be fined – and how many is "too many times"? If an Indian agent did not like an Indian then maybe one time was too many times.

> They made sure the Indians were off the streets after nine. We had a place to camp down by the stampede grounds.

This law snowballed and eventually many places did not allow Indians into their establishments at all. My grandmother used to talk about her niece working in the Famous Café in Williams Lake but Gram and my grandfather, *Xp'e7e* (Ba-ah), were only allowed to eat in the back of the café. Cecilia DeRose says, "We were allowed in Sin Tooie's Chinese Café. When we'd come to town twice a year for groceries, a cannon would go off at nine o'clock. They made sure the Indians were off the streets after nine. We had a place to camp down by the stampede grounds."

The only places Indians were allowed to frequent without any restrictions were premises where the Chinese people operated businesses. The Chinese and Aboriginal peoples formed great friendships. My grandmother talked about her good friends who lived by the river below her home community of Alexandria. They helped each other. When my mom and her husband were charged and later acquitted with murder in Wells, British Columbia, it was their Chinese friend, Old Wing, who gathered money from his family and friends and helped pay for the lawyer.

Because Aboriginal people were not allowed into the dance hall at the annual Williams Lake Stampede, "Squaw Hall" was set up as a place for Indians to dance. The Kamloops Thompson Valley Boys and later Hilary Place and his band provided great music. Despite the racist name, the older Aboriginal people have some very good memories of Squaw Hall. At that time people came from all over to attend the stampede. Even though the Indians were not allowed at the newcomer dances uptown, some of the newcomers came down to the Squaw Hall. They found they had more fun, and soon a huge number of newcomers came down. Eventually the dances that the Aboriginal people had enjoyed turned into wild free-for-alls. Many have memories of the year there was a bottle-throwing contest. Someone threw a bottle either in or out and someone threw one back. Soon bottles were being chucked back and forth over the roofless structure. Squaw Hall was eventually shut down in the mid-1970s because of the rowdiness and danger posed by some crazies. Cecilia DeRose laughingly says, "It got a little dangerous even for the Indians. The white man got too wild."

REMNANTS OF THE "No Indians Allowed" policy were still evident into the 1970s and 1980s. For example, my brother PeeWee went to a local drive-in restaurant in Williams Lake in the 1980s.

He pulled up outside and was looking at the menu above the car, thinking about what he and his family were going to order. A young server came out and told him, "We don't serve Indians here. You have to leave." My brother was rightfully so outraged and, knowing him, probably swore at the young woman. He left.

Another example, this one from my personal experience, happened in the late 1970s. When my children were about age three and four, my family went to the Quesnel rodeo. We went and bought some Kentucky Fried Chicken and were looking for a place to eat it. There was a campsite by the Quesnel River and we pulled in. We had not been to this campsite before but there were plenty of picnic tables and so we pulled up beside one and started to unload our meal onto the table. A newcomer came over and angrily told us to get out, "We don't want any Indians here!" he barked. I was young and still so unsecure and his obvious hatred could be seen and felt. I don't know if it was a private campsite or a government campsite but we left.

Even kids are not immune to this newcomer attitude. I was shopping in the local grocery store in Williams Lake when my son, Scott, was about eight or nine years old. I had shopped there before and didn't have any problems. On this particular day, Scott met up with a friend of his from school and they started to wander around the store. They were not doing anything wrong, just talking and laughing. Then they disappeared and didn't come back. I finished my shopping, kind of keeping an eye out for him, and went to pay. I took another look around the store but didn't see him. When I went outside, there he was standing by our truck. I said to him: "What are you doing? I was looking all over for you." He told me that some guy had approached him and told him that he couldn't stay in the store. Even though Scott responded saying that I was in the store shopping, he and his friend were told they would have to wait outside for me. I was so angry. I went into the store but whoever told him to wait outside was "not available" to meet with me. Later I phoned the store manager and tried to set up a meeting with him but that never happened.

Other Aboriginal people across Canada experience this kind of racial profiling all the time. One woman stood up to it. Gladys Johnston, a Cree from the Mistawasis reserve in Saskatchewan, had served in the Canadian Air Force during the Second World War and later was secretary treasurer of the Union of Saskatchewan Indians, as well as secretary to John G. Diefenbaker before he was prime minister. In 1961, she sat down in a restaurant in North Battleford and was told to leave because they "did not serve Indians." Johnston went to court and won – the owner was ordered to pay a $25 fine, according to Bob Burgel, who wrote about Johnston in a recent letter to the editor of the *Vancouver Sun*. "Canadians can learn from the courage of Gladys Johnston," Burgel wrote, "about how racism is part of our country's history, and how important it is to stand up to it."

THE 1927 AMENDMENT TO the Indian Act also introduced another new law oppressing Aboriginal human rights. It said that anyone taking money for Indian legal claims must first obtain a licence from the Department of Indian Affairs.

This law was to reduce the effectiveness of Indian leaders and organizations such as the Allied Tribes of British Columbia. They had already proven troublesome to the Department of Indian Affairs because of their insistence through letters and lobbying that their unresolved land issues be dealt with. Again notice who they put the restrictions on: any lawyers who wanted to do the work on an Indian legal claim would have to do it for free.

The effect of this provision was to prevent Indians all across Canada from hiring a lawyer to deal with their land issues. It allowed the government to illegally claim the lands without any interference and court challenges. This provision remained in effect until it was repealed in amendments to the Indian Act enacted in 1951. As a result the land issues of most nations in British Columbia and other parts of Canada are still outstanding.

BY THE TIME 1939 rolled around, Canada as a nation was involved in the second major conflict in the twentieth century. The Second World War was a time of great national pride, and Canadians of all backgrounds enlisted to fight for their country.

At the end of the Second World War, the Indian Affairs branch officially reported that more than three thousand status Indians had participated in the war, including seventy-two women and seven Indians from Yukon. One Aboriginal veterans group estimates that twelve thousand Natives served in the three wars, the Second World War under discussion, as well as the First World War before it and the Korean War following, but numbers are unknown because "some Indians and most Metis and Inuit were excluded from the Department of Indian Affairs tally." It is known that more than four thousand Aboriginal people, including Inuit, Metis, and status and non-status Indians, served in the First World War. Many Aboriginal soldiers were decorated with honours and awards and were highly praised for their skill and bravery.

Aboriginal languages played a crucial role during the wars. Most people are familiar with the Navajo code talkers in the Second World War, especially since the movie *Windtalkers*, starring Nicolas Cage and Adam Beach, was released in 2002. The U.S. Marine Corps specifically recruited the Navajo for the use of their language as a code to send crucial wartime messages. The enemy was never able to break the code, and the United States credits the Navajo as a big part of the reason the Allies won the war. The code talkers were forbidden from discussing their role even after the war ended, and it stayed a secret until recently.

In Canada the Cree language served the same purpose as the Navajo. Charles "Checker" Tompkins from Grouard, Alberta, along with other Cree soldiers, worked as a code talker during the Second World War. As a member of this special group his job was to translate military messages into Cree before they were sent out across European battlefields. Afterward the coded messages were received by another Aboriginal code talker, who translated them back into English and gave them to military officials to read. Often messages came from military officials requesting certain types of weapons for planned attacks, and it was vital that they remained cloaked from enemy ears.

The Aboriginal Peoples Television Network (APTN) recently aired a story about twenty-four Akwesasne Mohawk code talkers honoured for their role in the wars. APTN also reported: "According to New York Congresswoman Elise Stefanik, the St. Regis Mohawk tribe is one of thirty-three American Indian tribes being recognized for using their language to send coded messages." It is ironic that many of the Aboriginals who were recruited to use their language for the war effort were punished in their early years at the residential school for speaking it.

> The grinding thumb of the federal government that kept Aboriginal people down would soon lift with changes to the Indian Act. A light was appearing on the horizon.

ABORIGINAL SOLDIERS WERE treated as equals in war but it was a different story once they returned home. Not only did the Indian Act specify that any Indian absent from the reserve for four years was no longer a status Indian, but in order to sign up to fight in the Second World War, some Aboriginal soldiers had to relinquish Indian status and become enfranchised. These provisions meant that many Aboriginal veterans found, upon returning home after fighting overseas for Canada, they were no longer considered Indians. That meant they could no longer go home to live with their families on reserve. According to the Indian Act they would be trespassing and could be charged.

Those who were able to return to their communities did not have the right to other benefits available to non-Aboriginal veterans due to Indian Act restrictions. Aboriginal veterans on reserves in need of help were treated like other status Indians rather than as veterans. Many Second World War veterans, including Tommy George Prince, the most decorated Aboriginal war veteran, whose medals included the American Silver Star and six service medals, re-enlisted for the Korean War simply because they were unable to re-enter their previous existence. The lives of numerous Aboriginal veterans ended in despair and poverty.

Following the war in 1946, a joint committee of the House of Commons and Senate was convened to examine the Indian Act. The amendments that results would work to correct what had been the darkest period for Aboriginal people in Canada. From 1876 to the mid-twentieth century, in every way their efforts to thrive were being blocked. In the meantime, newcomers continued to arrive in this country to take advantage of the richness it promised. Their developments continued to gobble up the traditional territories of Aboriginal people. Racist laws kept the Aboriginal people out of sight and out of mind for most Canadians. The grinding thumb of the federal government that kept Aboriginal people down would soon lift with amendments to the Indian Act. A light was appearing on the horizon.

WHAT IF THE NEWCOMERS IGNORE YOUR HOUSE RULES AND IMPOSE THEIR OWN? DOES OWNERSHIP OF THE HOUSE TRANSFER WITHOUT YOUR CONSENT?

1951

Parliament amends the Indian Act to return many 1876 provisions

1960

Aboriginal people granted federal voting rights and phasing-out of residential schools begins

1960S AND 1970S

So many children are "scooped" that nearly one third of children in foster care and adoption are Aboriginal

Chapter Six

Political Action Renews

THE INDIAN ACT FROM 1951 FORWARD

1951 to 1969

I WAS BORN in 1955 and for the first five years of my life, like my mother and older relatives, I was not considered a citizen of Canada. Even after 1960 when federal and provincial votes were available to Aboriginal people, I followed the same path my ancestors were forced to walk: I was bullied, victimized, and traumatized by the state. Some of the more racist laws were removed in 1951 amendments to the Indian Act but, for the most part, it was business as usual for the Department of Indian Affairs and the federal and provincial governments. Nevertheless it was during this period that Aboriginal people were able to start openly organizing again to have their rights dealt with. The Aboriginal pushback grew in strength.

THE PRESENT-DAY INDIAN ACT is the result of the major revision that occurred in 1951. There have been changes since 1951, but it is generally accepted that the net effect of the 1951 revision was to return Canadian Indian legislation to its original form, as set out in the 1876 Indian Act. The increasingly repressive amendments since 1876 were repealed and as a result the 1876 and 1951 versions are very similar in essential respects. Much is still at the discretion of the minister.

One major amendment in 1951 was that the "half-day" system at residential schools was replaced with a full day of classes. Aboriginal children also began to be integrated into regular public schools. The 1951 amendments also removed restrictions on ceremonies. Aboriginal people could also now hire legal counsel, and women were given the vote in band council elections.

In 1951 other prohibitions in the Indian Act were repealed, including those that restricted political activity. Aboriginal people were able to resume the fight for their human rights without threat of being jailed. Aboriginal people could freely gather and discuss the issues and rights that they never abandoned. New Aboriginal political organizations began to emerge, with each province hosting its own political organizations. A national organization was founded that has morphed into the Assembly of First Nations to speak for on-reserve "Indians."

After 1951, blockades preventing access on railways, highways, and other public places raised awareness of Aboriginal issues. A few non-Aboriginals supported our cause but members of the general public for the most part were more annoyed than anything about the disruption in their daily lives. Many of these roadblocks slowed the "economy" as well. That made people angry but also got a lot of attention.

ANOTHER 1951 AMENDMENT allowed possession of liquor in a public place. In 1874 an amendment to the Indian Act had made it illegal for an Aboriginal person to be intoxicated on- or off-reserve; anyone found in this situation was punished with one month in jail. Failure to supply the name of the seller of the alcohol added another fourteen days in jail. After 1951 it was still against the law under the Indian Act for an Indian to be drinking off-reserve. So the Indian had to buy his or her alcohol and go back to the reserve to drink it. Many Indians served time in jail for being intoxicated off-reserve.

It got so that people did not even ask why someone went to jail. If anyone asked about someone who had been jailed, the response would be, "He (or she) went for a plane ride." (At that time Indians were on airplanes only when they went to jail.) When I was in the Wet'suwet'en area, they told me their saying was, "He (or she) went to pick potatoes." After an arrest there was no discussion about whether a person was innocent or not; it did not matter. This attitude was part of our hangover from the residential schools where you learned to accept whatever came your way whether you were innocent or not.

As a result of the increased awareness surrounding human rights after the Second World War, Canada established in 1960 the Canadian Bill of Rights, a law to protect individual freedoms and human rights. Joseph Drybones challenged the Indian Act under the new Canadian Bill of Rights when he was charged with being intoxicated off-reserve. Joseph Drybones lived in Yellowknife, Northwest Territories, where there were no Indian reserves. This meant that, as a status Indian, Joseph Drybones could buy liquor anywhere in the Northwest Territories. In order to legally drink it, however, he would have to take his liquor south to an Indian reserve in British Columbia, Alberta, or Saskatchewan, the closest reserve being situated a distance of more than five hundred kilometres away. Joseph Drybones challenged the 1874 amendment (which prohibited Aboriginal people from being intoxicated off-reserve) all the way to the Supreme Court of Canada before it was overturned in 1970. No non-Aboriginal could have been convicted of a similar offence. The Supreme Court of Canada decided that section 94(b) of the Indian Act was inoperative because it violated section 1(b) of the new Canadian Bill of Rights. As the judge stated, the prohibition infringed the "right of the respondent to equality before the law."

> Until 1951 only Indian men were allowed to vote in band elections. This had effectively removed Indian women from band political life.

OTHER SECTIONS OF the Indian Act had perpetuated inequality. Until 1951 only Indian men were allowed to vote in band elections. This had effectively removed Indian women from band political life. For matrilineal cultures this was devastating. Consider, for example, Bill's mom and the effect this provision had on her. Bill's dad, Charlie Wilson, did not have clan status within his nation; he was a commoner. So when Bill's mom married Charlie, though her high-ranking status did not change within the Aboriginal community, it changed under the Indian Act, which since 1876 had reduced the status of women upon marriage and still despite the 1951 amendments continued to diminish women's status.

Another example is what happened to me. When I married in 1975, I was shocked to find out that I, along with my two children, had automatically been transferred to the Bella Coola Indian Band because that is where my husband was registered. I was not Nuxalkmc and did not have any rights in their traditional community. The Department of Indian Affairs did not consult the Nuxalkmc people about whether they would accept me. The Department of Indian Affairs did not consult me even though my life was solidly set in my home community. In an instant I lost all rights I had in my Secwepemc community. Thankfully my then husband agreed to transfer to Soda Creek and my children and I automatically followed in accordance with the Indian Act. I love my Nuxalk relatives but my home was sacred to me and yet I had absolutely no control over my destiny.

Women have always been leaders whether they were elected or not. Adele Sellars was known as the Grandmother of Soda Creek. She was the one everyone went to for advice or help of some kind. She was always there for the community no matter who they were. When the Indian Act was changed and women were allowed to vote, she was elected. It just verified her role in the community for the non-Natives. Addie even hosted Jean Chrétien in her house when he was Minister of Indian Affairs. She treated him well, as she did everyone else who crossed her threshold.

I was making a statement to someone about how women's active involvement in band poltics was a non-issue. Donna Dixon, who is now chief of Xat'súll, added, "It would be an issue if women did *not* run for chief or council." She is right. If by chance an all-male list were put forward, *that* would be something to talk about.

When our tribal council first brought the residential-schools issue to light in the late 1980s, a non-Aboriginal person told me, "Now we will have to get the women's liberation movement happening in the Native communities." Women's liberation was not an Aboriginal issue until the newcomers forcibly changed our social structures. We have social problems in our communities but they do not stem from the historical notion that women are seen as the property of men. Some ill-informed Aboriginal men accepted the Indian Act's denial of rights to women but traditionally this was not an issue.

UNFORTUNATELY THE FALLOUT from the denial of rights to women has been devastating. A report released by the Royal Canadian Mounted Police in 2014 marks the first time that police in Canada have attempted, at the national level, to identify how many First Nations, Inuit, and Metis women and girls have been murdered or have gone missing – a problem that has been common knowledge in affected communities for many years. According to the report, 1,017 women and girls identified as Aboriginal were murdered between 1980 and 2012 – a homicide rate roughly four and a half times higher than that of all other women in Canada.

Society has its hierarchy and these women do not matter much to any of the authorities, as evidenced by the case of Robert Pickton. In the 1990s, Pickton was murdering mostly Aboriginal women in Vancouver's Downtown Eastside, and there is evidence that some on the streets knew who was responsible and tried to report him. This information was ignored because the women sources mostly lived in the part of town where the "down-and-out" live. It took years, and more women lost their lives before the information was taken seriously. Pickton was eventually convicted with six murders but most people believe he is responsible for as many as forty-nine.

The Downtown Eastside is a neighbourhood in Vancouver where many Aboriginal people live; in fact, some of the *Kekewes e Muts* – as we call members of the Secwepemc Nation who are away from home – now live there. I heard someone once say that if they had to be dropped off in Vancouver without knowing anyone, they would want to be dropped off in the Downtown Eastside. They were convinced that if they were dropped off there, they were guaranteed that someone would reach out to them; but if they were dropped off in the richer parts of town, no one would even open the door to them.

A perfect example is the time my mom made an unexpected trip to the Downtown Eastside. She had gone to the Pacific National Exhibition, and though I was to pick her up later, she decided she would take the city bus back to our apartment. Mom was in her eighties by this time and still "never wanted to bother anyone," another aspect of our hangover from residential school. Mom accidentally got off the bus on East Hastings Street, where all the people gather. It must have been obvious that she was lost. A lady came up to her and asked if she needed help. Mom confirmed that she didn't know where she was and that she couldn't see a payphone to use to call me. The lady stood by Mom and helped her find someone who had a cellphone. They called and the lady told me where to find her, then stayed with Mom until I got there. I can't imagine what Mom would have done if the lady had not helped her. I was so grateful that Mom got off the bus in the right part of the city.

INEQUALITIES BEGAN TO be addressed in the 1951 amendments but some didn't go quite far enough. Although the Aboriginal vote was considered, it wasn't until 1960 that Aboriginal people could finally vote in federal elections. In 1948, a parliamentary committee had recommended the vote be extended to Aboriginal people, and the Inuit were enfranchised that year. First Nations in British Columbia were able to vote in provincial elections beginning in 1949.

That year, Bill's brother, Rusty Wilson, was going to school at the University of British Columbia. Rusty was politically active but up to that time he didn't have a vote. Colin Cameron was Rusty's best friend and also a descendant of the original creators of the Co-operative Commonwealth Federation (CCF), the precursor to the New Democratic Party (NDP). Rusty was a member of the Native Brotherhood of British Columbia. In 1949, when Colin told Rusty the provincial government had just passed legislation to allow Indians to vote, Colin said that they should go to Atlin, British Columbia's northern-most community, and get someone to run because the majority of people in that northern electoral district, Skeena, were Native. Rusty said they didn't need to go as far as Atlin; only needed to walk across campus to the Anglican theological college where Frank Calder was studying. Frank was born in the Nass River Valley in the riding of Skeena. He agreed to run and won the nomination and election as the first Aboriginal person to occupy a parliamentary or legislative seat in the British parliamentary system.

For the federal vote, a strong argument has been made by Roland Chrisjohn of the Oneida Nation that Aboriginal people got the franchise in 1960 so they would not take Canada to international court for genocide. After the Second World War with the extermination of six million Jewish people, the international community got together and said that the world could never allow such a thing to happen again. They came up with the Genocide Convention but in order to pass it they had to define *genocide* and so a list was drawn up.

The 1948 Convention on the Prevention and Punishment of the Crime of Genocide or the "Genocide Convention," Article 2(e), declares that the forcible transfer of children from a protected group to another group is an act that amounts to genocide when it is conducted "with intent to destroy" the group "as such," at least "in part" by "forcibly removing children and raising them in a foreign environment." These terms clearly described the residential schools in Canada, and because the last residential schools did not close until the 1990s, Canada was in clear violation of the Genocide Convention.

Chrisjohn contends that Canada avoided this argument by turning to an international law, the Act of State Doctrine, which states that "a Nation is sovereign within its own borders and its domestic actions may not be questioned in the courts of another nation." Canada realized that if they gave the Indians voting rights, then the residential-schools issue would become a domestic issue and the Indians would not be able to take the government of Canada to international court.

Aboriginal people were given the vote only after all the laws and policies that now govern their traditional lands were enacted. This was an extreme violation of our human rights.

BY 1967 THE law had changed again and it was no longer required for Indian children to attend residential schools. Although the last residential schools were not closed until the 1990s, by the mid-1980s it was widely and publicly recognized that the residential schools and the foster-home experience, like the deadly diseases, had devastated and continued to devastate Aboriginal communities.

Residential schools were the most destructive to Aboriginal people but other tools were used to try to eradicate, in one way or another, the original inhabitants of this land. Like many other Aboriginal children, I was taken and placed in a residential school where I was always hungry, scared, lonely, and made to do more labour than a child should be expected to do at that age. Most residential schools were closed in the 1980s and Aboriginal children integrated into public schools; however, that often brought unsolicited judgment of Aboriginal families, and Children and Family Services was often called to apprehend children who school administrators believed were not adequately cared for.

From the 1960s to the late 1980s a large number of Aboriginal children were fostered by, or adopted into non-Aboriginal families in North America and Europe. This policy and its aftermath are now refered to as the *Sixties Scoop*. It is hard to determine the exact number of Aboriginal children taken, but some – among them Ernie Crey from the Stó:lō Nation who, with journalist Suzanne Fournier, wrote the award-winning examination of this issue titled *Stolen from Our Embrace* – estimate it could be as high as twenty thousand. It didn't matter if the child was cared for in a safe home with good food and a loving family. The determining factor was that the child was Aboriginal and therefore his or her parents and grandparents were not fit to raise their own children. I won't get into too much discussion of the Sixties Scoop here because that is an experience I do not have. I refer to it because it is part of the history that needs to be known. There are many who can speak to that particular experience. Ernie Crey and also Cindy Blackstock are great starting points.

Instead, I can speak to my own experience, in particular, when I was in hospital with my firstborn, Jacinda, not long after her birth in 1974. The nurse came to me with a pen and some papers for me to sign. I asked her what they were and she said, "Adoption papers." I panicked and got very upset, thinking they were going to make me sign away my daughter. Only then did the nurse back down, saying, "Okay, okay. We just thought you might want to give the baby up." *At no time* had I indicated to anyone that I was thinking of giving up my child. It makes me wonder how many other Aboriginal girls lost their babies that way.

Many children were apprehended and adopted out to non-Aboriginal families, including Cameron Kerley, a young Cree who brutally murdered his American adoptive father. Turns out the adoptive father had been sexually abusing Cameron for years. It became apparent that Cameron had been failed by the child-welfare systems of both Canada and the United States. Instead of trying to find someone in Cameron's extended family to take him and his three siblings, Canada allowed him to be adopted out to a single father in the United States. Once adopted, no one from either country checked to see how Cameron was doing and whether the adoptive home was suitable for the young boy. It resulted in a murder, and Cameron was convicted and sentenced to a minimum of fifteen years in prison. Eventually U.S. authorities allowed him to return to Manitoba to serve his sentence.

I also remember watching a documentary about an Aboriginal girl who had been "scooped" to England. She too had been sexually abused by her adoptive father and as an adult ended up on the streets. As a young adult she read a news article about a group of Canadian Aboriginal chiefs visiting London to try to get their grievances dealt with by the Queen's officials. The young woman went to the place the chiefs were meeting and burst in on them: "I don't know what nation I am from but I know I am one of you. Please help me to go home!" The chiefs did help her, and she found her way back to her people in Canada.

I RECENTLY HEARD a story about the horrible conditions of orphanages in England many years ago. I felt sorry for those poor kids and then I started to think about traditional Aboriginal societies. It dawned on me that orphanages, which seemed to be quite common in Europe, did not exist in traditional Aboriginal communities. Children were precious and belonged to everyone. They were *our children*, not *my* children. It was expected that if a child lost his or her parents for whatever reason, the extended family would step in and make sure the child remained a part of the community. It was an obligation on the part of the nation to care for the children just as it was an obligation to care for the elderly, for example. We all had an obligation to look after one another. It was also an obligation for family, if a couple could not bear children, to give them one of their own. In our community, that practice was still in place as recently as forty years ago. There are at least two examples in my community of this practice. Even though the two babies had capable biological parents, they were given to those who had no children.

> The residential schools and the Sixties Scoop are still in effect, just in a different form.

Growing up, when I was home from residential school, every member of the community looked out for me. If I needed discipline, I got it from any older person and I could not run home to complain to anyone; that just was not done. But it wasn't physical punishment I received, just a few words of wisdom. When I was in high school, a newcomer doing research told me that Secwepemc people never hit their children. It was the first time I learned anything about my culture that was written about in books, and it gave me such a sense of pride. Now things have changed so much in our communities.

Today we have remnants of a government administration that thinks the Aboriginal nations need to be overseen. The residential schools and the Sixties Scoop are still in effect, just in a different form. In the 1980s, delegated child-care agencies were implemented, via Indigenous Affairs and Northern Development Canada National Policy Directive 20-1, as an interim measure for on-reserve First Nations child and family services. The goal was to reduce the number of Native children in government care – but that goal has still not been reached. Legal advisor Jay Nelson attributes this failure to the delegated agency being "crisis oriented and focused on the child in isolation; it does not address the root causes of child maltreatment in Aboriginal communities; it is inadequately financed; and it does not truly reflect Aboriginal cultural values or empower Aboriginal decision-making."

In March 2009, our seventeen Secwepemc chiefs hosted a forum in Kamloops to discuss the revival of jurisdiction and authority over the nations' member children and families in the traditional territory. The chiefs' vision was to improve the health and social outcomes for nation members by advancing strategies that would ensure the survival, dignity, and well-being of the people and to reduce the number of children in government care while supporting their cultural connection. At the forum, the seventeen chiefs signed a declaration to collectively work in unity to accomplish this goal. The Stemémelt Secwepemc Nation Project had begun.

Doreen Johnson, a Secwepemc community member, was hired in March 2010 as the project's executive director. Chiefs met on a regular basis and a lot of good work has been done. Other nations also worked to regain jurisdiction over their children. However, in November 2013, the Representative for Children and Youth for British Columbia released a report that did not reflect well on Aboriginal child-service organizations, and the Stemémelt project along with all the other tribal projects were shut down. The Secwepemc people were unsuccessful in regaining control of our children, and the Ministry of Children and Family became once again the caretakers of our nation's children.

The removal of Aboriginal children from their natural families is evidence of a blatant clash of cultural values. Across Canada, Aboriginal parents traditionally shared common methods of raising children. They were the heart of the community and everyone played a role in raising and nurturing them. Native children were encouraged to learn from and explore their natural world. Meanwhile, many newcomers disapprovingly remarked that Native people allowed our children to run free.

I WAS VERY fortunate to be born at the tail end of this type of child rearing. While we were home from residential school for summer holidays, a group of kids would spend all day out in the bush, fishing, riding horses, or just exploring. Sometimes we would leave early in the morning and get home just before dark. This was totally acceptable to my grandparents. As long as we were with older, more experienced kids and the ever-present guard dog to warn us of any danger, my grandparents never worried about us being away for long periods of time. We were very comfortable in the bush and were unafraid of dangers that might be lurking nearby. When we did see a wild animal, it was usually running away from us.

My children grew up in the remnants of this atmosphere of freedom-based child rearing as well. My daughter, Jacinda, went on a student exchange trip to Portugal for a full year. One of the things she had a hard time accepting while she was away was the discipline expected, particularly when inviting friends over. In our community if a friend does not have a place to stay, you simply take him or her home with you. No questions asked. But in Portugal, Jacinda got into trouble a number of times for bringing friends home without asking first. She found it hard to accept that when a friend needed help, she couldn't just do the natural thing.

During my son Scott's teenage years, he travelled mostly with the same group of boys who came from communities near and far. I would ask them who their parents were and from their answers I knew all I needed to know about them, their nation, their community, and who they were related to. If there was a strange one every now and again, the kid usually knew to introduce himself by naming his parents and grandparents. If he just told me his personal name, that meant nothing to me. If he told me his lineage, then I knew automatically who he was and just as quickly a bond or connection formed between us.

Scott and his friends played hockey together and many times on weekends or during the summer months I would wake up in the morning to find teenagers sprawled all over the living room. They would arrive through the night, eat, and then sleep. The next day they got up, fed themselves, and carried on to the next house. No questions asked. It was simply accepted in all Aboriginal homes that this sharing of space and care was part of having children. It was also expected that as long as these kids were respectful, they had a number of homes they could invade for a night or two.

My youngest son, Tony, did his share of roaming in his very early years. There were about six houses in the community that Tony stayed at on a regular basis. By the time he was four or five, he had already established himself in each of these houses. He would leave my house with one of my relatives and be gone for days, usually making his rounds to different houses. Every now and again I would get a glimpse of him riding in the back of a truck or hanging with his relatives on the rez. "Hi, Mom!" he would holler as he zoomed by. I never worried about him unless I hadn't heard from him in three or four days. Usually he would phone and let me know if he had changed houses but every now and again he would forget. It didn't take me long to track him down and eventually, when he was ready, he would come home. In our small community, I knew whether a home was safe or not, and sometimes I would not allow Tony to be in certain homes until the drinking stopped. If this were to happen today, I am sure Children and Family Services would have something to say and might apprehend my children. They still interfere and impose their failed solutions even when they don't know the inner workings of an Aboriginal community.

In my community growing up it was not uncommon for an elder to discipline me with words if I needed it. It was accepted that if a child needed a stern talking-to, whoever was closest would deliver those words. I remember being scolded by a number of different elders, both men and women, and I took it as seriously as if it had been my grandparents who had scolded me. That culture in our community no longer exists because of the many impositions of outsiders on our methods of raising children. Now people are scared to say anything to kids who are not directly related to them.

> Taking children away from their culture and raising them in a foreign environment failed miserably then and continues to fail today.

Newcomers on the other hand feel completely free to comment on the way Aboriginal people raise their children, and their words have serious consequences for personal health and well-being. For example, my grandmother, like many Aboriginal people, rarely went to the doctor unless it was to see Dr. Lee, the only Chinese doctor in town. Gram did not seek the services of a doctor until at age eighty-eight she had such tremendous pain in her knee that she finally agreed to seek help. All her experiences with doctors had been negative. She was still bitter when she told me of her daughter

Janet who died when she was only twelve years old. Janet suffered severe headaches and the Indian medicines did not help, so Gram, in desperation, went to see a doctor in Williams Lake. Gram said she was so upset when the doctor told Gram that the only thing the matter with Janet was that Gram gave her too much coffee. Gram did not allow her kids to drink coffee. She was angry that the doctor would blame the coffee, but she didn't say anything and took Janet home. Later the headaches got so bad that Gram had to take her to the hospital. Janet ended up dying during the night. The next day, Gram went back to the hospital and they told her that her daughter was dead because of a brain tumour. The girl in the bed next to Janet told Gram that no one had done anything for Janet. Apparently, they had not even given her an Aspirin for her headaches. Gram always felt guilty and angry for leaving Janet in the hospital. She said that if Janet were home, at least she would have been able to attend to her and try to make her comfortable. She hated that Janet died in pain and with no one around to comfort her.

Newcomers often feel free to comment on the way Aboriginal people raise their children. They do not agree with our child-rearing practices and, as in other culture clashes, legislation has been set up to try to "correct" the way Aboriginal people raise their children. Through a series of government policies and the Indian Act, our traditional systems have been undermined. Taking children away from their culture and raising them in a foreign environment failed miserably then and continues to fail today.

WE HAD THE OPPORTUNITY at one point to get rid of the Indian Act. This was when Pierre Elliott Trudeau was prime minister and Jean Chrétien was his minister of Indian affairs. In 1969 they came up with the "White Paper" that rejected the concept of special status for Aboriginal people within Confederation. They said that because Canada was a "Just Society," the government should remove distinctions between Indians and other Canadians. That included doing away with any treaties that Canada had with the

Aboriginal nations. The government argued that Aboriginal and treaty rights were irrelevant in today's society.

The responses from Aboriginal political organizations were numerous. An important one came from Harold Cardinal and the Indian Association of Alberta, who retaliated with their paper "Citizens Plus" or the "Red Paper." Harold later wrote a detailed book on Aboriginal issues in Canada, *The Unjust Society*. Bill said that every young Native leader of his era carried Cardinal's book around as their bible. It was one of the first renowned books written about Aboriginal issues by an Aboriginal person.

The National Indian Brotherhood held meetings about the White Paper and Aboriginal people across Canada let their intense displeasure be known. Eventually Trudeau and Chrétien withdrew the White Paper.

AT ABOUT THAT time in the early 1970s the American Indian Movement (AIM) came to Canada very briefly. I was a young mother at the time and our then chief came back from a political meeting informing us that there might be drive-by shootings in our community. I had seen the news broadcasts about the Pine Ridge Indian Reservation in the United States and the political turmoil there. I saw children crying and some screaming from fright. I had two small children at the time and thinking of them having to go through the same experience scared the heck out of me. That was definitely not the future I envisioned for my children.

The Pine Ridge Indian Reservation came to international attention in February 1973 when a group of two hundred American Indian Movement activists took control of Wounded Knee, South Dakota, a tiny town, where in 1890, the U.S. Cavalry opened fire on and massacred the Lakota Nation in an attempt to steal their land. Historian Dee Brown, in *Bury My Heart at Wounded Knee*, reported more than three hundred died in that attack. The American Indian Movement occupation at Wounded Knee in 1973 marked the beginning of three years of political violence between

FBI agents and traditional tribal leaders and AIM members. One AIM leader implicated in the murder of FBI agents was Leonard Peltier, who fled to Canada to escape prosecution. While in Canada, Bill's family tried to protect Peltier from extradition. This chapter closes with the story Bill tells.

LEONARD PELTIER IS MY BROTHER

Leonard Peltier was adopted by my mother, Ethel Pearson (Puugladee), matriarch of the Musgamagw, at a potlatch in Gwaysdumes, the village where my mother spent most of her summers.

My sister, Donna Tyndall, was an activist in many causes. She went down to Wounded Knee during the American Indian Movement protests. During this time she got to know the Indian leaders involved, including Leonard Peltier.

Leonard was a warrior, a long-time defender of the land, the resources, and his people. Later Leonard would be charged with the shooting of two FBI agents, a sad result of the sickening attempt by the FBI, the U.S. Army, and the U.S. federal government to put down legitimate Native Indian protests.

Donna informed me that the FBI, the U.S. Army, and the American government responded to the legitimate Indian protests over land and resources by basically declaring war against the Indians in South Dakota. They brought in armoured vehicles, tanks, even jet fighters to put down a few armed warriors.

Leonard fled to Canada after the alleged shooting incident. He was harboured here by many people and then finally arrested. He was held in the old Oakalla Prison Farm where fifty years earlier my grandfather, Hemas Kla-Lee-Lee-Kla, had been incarcerated for practising his potlatch. Donna became an integral part of the Leonard Peltier Defence Committee and, in the vainglorious hope that Leonard's extradition to the United States could be prevented, convinced

Law enforcement officers with a handcuffed Leonard Peltier, February 6, 1976.
PHOTO by Bettmann

my mother, Ethel Pearson, to adopt him in our potlatch way. The rationale was that adoption in Canada would prevent Peltier's extradition to the United States.

Leonard, of course, was not able to attend the potlatch and remained behind bars in Oakalla while his extradition was being considered by the federal government. It turned out that the then justice minister, the Honourable Ron Basford, had grown up in Comox, was a friend of my brothers, and spent a great deal of time at my mother's house. My mother had known him since he was a child.

At the insistence of Donna and the Defence Committee, Mom journeyed to Ottawa to plead with Justice Minister Basford not to extradite Leonard to the United States. These efforts proved futile and Leonard was ultimately transferred from Oakalla to the U.S. prison system. He was tried in what can only be described as a kangaroo court and convicted of two murder charges and sentenced to life imprisonment on each charge.

I had the privilege of meeting my brother Leonard Peltier only once. He was behind bullet-proof glass in the Oakalla Prison Farm and we had to speak to each other by telephone. We were allowed less than twenty minutes yet I was impressed with his obvious commitment to the struggle of Native Indian people and his strength even while in the shackles of the white man's prison system.

My mother had instructed me to deliver an authentic Cowichan Indian sweater to Leonard which, of course, had to be examined by the guards before he could wear it. I watched his exit from Oakalla, shackled and bound at the feet and wrists. He was loaded onto a helicopter to fly to the United States proudly wearing the sweater my mother gave him.

Despite all the efforts of the Defence Committee, lobbying by other national and international agencies, as well as the fact that his co-defendant was finally acquitted, Leonard has remained in federal penitentiaries for the past forty years.

A young man taken in the prime of his life began his incarceration in an old federal penitentiary at Leavenworth, Kansas. What a price to pay for being a fighter for freedom and a warrior on behalf of Native Indian people, the land, and the resources.

Leonard, like all Aboriginal people in North, Central, and South America, has paid enough for trying to defend and preserve ourselves as a distinct race of people in a land that once belonged entirely to us.

—HEMAS KLA-LEE-LEE-KLA
(Hereditary Chief Bill Wilson)

WHAT IF THE NEWCOMERS FINALLY
AGREE TO SIT DOWN AND TALK?
SHOULD THEIR OPINIONS ABOUT
OWNERSHIP BE MORE VALID?

1982

Constitution Act acknowledges Aboriginal rights

1983

Inaugural First Ministers' Conference on the
Rights of Aboriginal Peoples

1985

Second Conference on the Rights of Aboriginal
Peoples

Chapter Seven

Aboriginal Leaders and First Ministers

CONSTITUTIONAL CONFERENCE ON ABORIGINAL AFFAIRS

BY HEMAS KLA-LEE-LEE-KLA (HEREDITARY CHIEF BILL WILSON)

March 15 and 16, 1983

Bill had a part in the one and only amendment made to Canada's constitution in 1982 and because he was there it is better to have him write about it. The following chapter is in Bill's words.

BY THE EARLY 1980s, Pierre Elliott Trudeau had repatriated the Canadian constitution. Many Aboriginal leaders managed to have Aboriginal issues discussed on the constitutional agenda, and as a result, Aboriginal rights were acknowledged in section 35 of the Constitution Act, 1982. In March 1983, I and other Native leaders met with then Prime Minister Pierre Elliott Trudeau to discuss further amendments to the constitution supporting Aboriginal rights at a First Ministers' Conference in Ottawa. We eventually succeeded, and a constitutional amendment was passed and approved guaranteeing Aboriginal and treaty rights.

A second constitutional conference was scheduled for the following year, and during the time in between, the Joint Standing

Committee on Indian Self-Government of the House of Commons and the Senate examined ways of getting free of the Indian Act and assuming self-government. Fifty-eight recommendations were made and the major one was getting rid of the Indian Act and how to do that. Headed by Keith Penner, a member of Parliament from Ontario, the committee had travelled all over the United States to examine self-government options and saw how they were working. It was the first official recognition that Aboriginal peoples have their own legitimate form of political institutions.

By the spring or early summer of 1982, I had become the vice-president of the Native Council of Canada (now the Congress of Aboriginal Peoples). Louis "Smokey" Bruyere, president of the Native Council of Canada, asked me if I wanted to be on the committee. Bruyere explained what it was and I agreed to sit on it. In May or June 1983, I started travelling with the committee, which went everywhere in Canada. The committee of twenty-four to thirty people (only eight or nine MPs and senators plus ex-officio members) would fly into a community, check into accommodation, and then hold meetings in band offices and community halls, listening to people make presentations on self-government. I would always begin by saying: "In my territory in the old days we had the system of the potlatch," then describe the self-government aspects of this traditional ceremony, and close with the question, "What did you have?" It was a breakthrough because it responded to the constitutional change that resulted from the constitutional conference of 1983. The resulting report, called the Penner Report, was tabled in House of Commons in October 1983. It was accepted – and then went away. Those fifty-eight recommendations, if acted upon, would have changed the life of the Aboriginal people. Here's how it all happened.

> It was the first official recognition that Aboriginal peoples have their own legitimate form of political institutions.

AFTER TEN MONTHS OF PREPARATION across the country the Aboriginal leaders spent a whole month in Ottawa before the March 1983 conference. It was for me an exhausting time sitting through meetings and hearing so many Indian leaders just make the same old speeches.

Fortunately a core group of Aboriginal people knew the importance and opportunity of the process. It was worse than pulling teeth to try to get one's own group together. Combine that with the Inuit, the Indian, and the then two Metis groups – each had multiple egos – and the problem became enormous. Somehow we managed to solve it and go forward with at least a publicly unified voice.

The night before the conference the representatives of the Indian, Inuit, and Metis peoples along with the prime minister, the premiers, and their senior officials were hosted by the Governor General at Rideau Hall. It was the first time I had ever been there and the formality of the seating arrangements rather surprised me. Everything was arranged according to "importance" or Confederation precedence. The prime minister sat at the head table with the leaders of the Indian organizations, and the rest of us were ranked according to elected status.

Bob Stevenson, a Metis representative from the Northwest Territories, and I took a cab to Rideau Hall, where the entrance swarmed with TV cameras, Klieg lights, and reporters. Bob was wearing a Native buckskin jacket and being someone who hates suits and ties I was dressed casually. As Bob and I approached the crush of reporters, I heard one ask his assistant, "Who the hell are these guys?" "Nobody!" his assistant replied.

I could see Bob's anger rising so I grabbed his arm and took him past the reporters before he could make a scene. In the foyer of Rideau Hall I told Bob, "Don't worry about it. They may not know who we are now but they certainly will when this conference is over."

We went through the reception line shaking hands with other officials and at the end the Governor General, Ed Schreyer, whom I had met a few times when he was premier of Saskatchewan. Bob and I sat at separate tables and I had the great pleasure of sitting next to René Lévesque, then premier of Quebec. The tables were set with the most expensive silverware I have ever seen. Each seat had an embossed nameplate. There were twelve seats, eight special guests, and four aide-de-camps all in full dress uniform, all fluently bilingual.

I looked around the room and noticed that Bob Stevenson and I were the only ones in the place not dressed in suits. Even the other Metis, Indian, and Inuit leaders all wore suits. I suppose that is the way it is but I simply never liked uniforms.

Premier René Lévesque apparently was notorious for being late and he arrived in a cloud of smoke, in a rumpled suit that looked like it had been slept in. He found his seat next to mine and picked up my nameplate. With an exaggerated francophone accent he said, "Beel Weelson." I picked up his nameplate, looked at him and said, "Reen-ie Lavesca?" Lévesque took a drag on his cigarette, extended his hand, and said, "I like you already."

> Lévesque took a drag on his cigarette, extended his hand, and said, "I like you already."

This was back in the bad old smoking days. In front of each guest was a silver candelabrum holder with ten cigarettes. After sitting down, Lévesque picked up his candelabrum and dumped the cigarettes into his jacket pocket. He then asked me if I smoked, and when I told him I did not he picked up mine and dumped it into his other pocket. "First f***ing thing I have ever gotten free from the federal government," he said to me and laughed.

In my political career I have met every premier since W.A.C. Bennett and every prime minister since Lester B. Pearson. I have to say that René Lévesque had the greatest personality of all the non-Aboriginal politicians I have ever met. He was truly fun to be around. I realized over time that he and Pierre Elliott Trudeau were the two most intellectually brilliant white politicians I have ever met.

Only one person at the table of twelve did not speak French. I do not pretend to speak French fluently but all the time I spent in Ottawa and Montreal gave me the ability to understand and respond. The conversation therefore took place mainly in French.

The intergovernmental affairs minister from Alberta, Jim Horsman, complained to me about not understanding the conversation even though he had an aide-de-camp fluent in both languages sitting next to him. Mr. Horsman irritated Mr. Lévesque by trying to insist that we all speak English. Mr. Lévesque with a cigarette in each hand continued to speak French and said to me as an aside in his perfect French diction, "It's true he really is a horse's ass, isn't he."

Mr. Horsman stuck his finger across the table and demanded that I translate what had been said. Trying not to laugh I came up with, "Mr. Lévesque thinks that your name suits you." Fortunately the dinner then adjourned. I shook hands with Mr. Lévesque and got out of there as quickly as possible. The last I saw of him he was emptying candelabra filled with cigarettes from the place settings of other non-smokers.

THE FIRST DAY OF THE first constitutional conference with Aboriginal people took place in the old railway station in Ottawa on March 15, 1983.

I was staying across the street at the Chateau Laurier and only had to go through the tunnel to get to the meeting hall. I got there fifteen minutes late. Fortunately Prime Minister Pierre Elliott Trudeau was twenty minutes late. He had been delayed opening the new Rideau Centre (a shopping mall) just down the street.

This conference was the result of more than ten months of official meetings across the country held with representatives of the provincial governments, territorial governments, federal governments, and the Indian, Inuit, and Metis peoples. A sixteen-item agenda formed the basis of the discussions.

Prime Minister Trudeau began the meeting by stating his government's position and then the Aboriginal people were allowed to speak. There followed an exchange dominated by certain negative and very uninformed provincial premiers. It was apparent to me that only the Aboriginal people and the federal government had done their homework. Even some of the Aboriginal reps were not aware of the high stakes for which we were playing. I and others knew that we had the chance to make a constitutional amendment, which we did.

One thing I did not know is that the two full days of the conference were being broadcast live across the country by CBC TV. I had thought only the introductions would go out as news clips.

Even though I am a status Indian, I was representing a non-status Metis group as the vice-president of the Native Council of Canada. I had an argument with a status Indian representative from the National Indian Brotherhood and Assembly of First Nations. I did not want the disagreement to emerge on the floor so I asked this fellow to go for a short walk with me at lunch time in order to clear the air between us.

We walked to the War Memorial and back and I was surprised at the response from the public. We had only been on national television for a few minutes each, yet both of us were recognized and received with handshakes, congratulations, and praise for our input.

The Aboriginal leaders, the prime minister, Premier Lévesque, and Premier Richard Hatfield from New Brunswick were the only ones who had a clue about the importance of the discussions. Certain premiers viewed the conference as an opportunity to be negative and blame Aboriginal people for their own problems. It was clear that they viewed the conference simply as a show of "power and who exercises it." Sadly even some of the Aboriginal leaders saw it only as an opportunity to dress up and get their faces on television.

I cannot leave the subject of the constitutional conference without commending certain individuals. I have already mentioned Prime Minister Trudeau, Lévesque, and Richard Hatfield but the ones who really knocked me out with their brilliance were the Indian, Inuit, and Metis leaders. To mention any one is to exclude some, but I have to say that James Gosnell, Jim Sinclair, Zebedee Nungak,

John Amagoalik, Mary Simon, and Joe Mathias proved themselves superior to the mostly rag-tag bunch of uninformed premiers.

The 1983 constitutional amendment has formed the basis of all successful Aboriginal court cases since it was enshrined. The recognition in the highest law of the non-Aboriginal people has been used by Aboriginal people to put forward their claims successfully.

From complete denial and refusal to even negotiate or in any way discuss Aboriginal title, we have come to a point at which the courts and most newcomer governments recognize that the Aboriginal people must be heard with regard to their historic land and human rights grievances.

We are very close to realizing James Gosnell's statement that we own the land "lock, stock, and barrel." While this will never be recognized by non-Aboriginal governments, the fact is that Aboriginal people require informed consent before natural resource projects can be developed. Nation-to-nation relationships should be the basis of all understandings and form the foundation of mutual respect and dignity among all Canadians.

Sadly the Indian Act and its incompetent bureaucracy still stand in the way of progress but we now have a government that seems committed to dealing fairly with the Aboriginal peoples across this country.

The 1983 constitutional conference was a historic event that actually changed the power position for Aboriginal peoples in this country.

THE MARCH 1983 constitutional conference was convened as the first of four required under the constitution patriation agreement with England. This conference was the first to be held with the Aboriginal leaders, the premiers, and the prime minister. It produced the first, and still to date the only, amendment to Canada's newly patriated constitution.

The amendment reads under section 35(1) "existing Aboriginal Title and Treaty Rights shall hereby be recognized and affirmed."

This section was protected by section 25(1) of the Charter of Rights and Freedoms, the so-called "non-obstante" clause, which was required to have section 35 protected from court cases alleging inequality with other Canadians.

The stage for the conference had been set by a process led by the Metis, Inuit, and Indian Leaders who actually travelled to London to create a lobby to ensure that conditions be added by the British Parliament to the patriation legislation. These conditions were designed to protect the interests of the Aboriginal people in Canada who had never before been consulted in regard to the British North America Act and the legal and legislative authority that had governed Canada since 1867.

> The 1983 constitutional amendment would become the solid platform on which all future court cases would be built.

Chief Del Riley, Harry Daniels, and other Aboriginal leaders travelled to England and successfully argued for the conditions of the patriation, which took place in April 1982 when the constitution was "brought home." The Aboriginal leaders, the provincial and territorial governments, and the federal government were given a year to prepare for the constitutional conference.

There followed a year-long process that included meeting at some level nearly every week. Senior official meetings took place monthly. While I was not part of the London lobby, I did attend most of the preparatory meetings. It was pure coincidence or karma that I should be involved in any way. I had desired to quit Indian politics after thirty years in order to practise law and make some real money. My good friend Bob Warren convinced me to go to Ottawa, where I was elected vice-president of the Native Council of Canada.

Strangely, it had also happened that Constitutional Law was the only course that I really enjoyed in law school. I realized later that even though I did not know it, I had been preparing all my life for this role in Aboriginal historic development.

My parents took me to Native Brotherhood of British Columbia meetings when I was very young. The words I heard there over and over again were "land claims." The NBBC was the pioneer organization in the pursuit of land claims, the attempt to regain control of our land, resources, and our lives as Indian people in our own right.

I had the distinct privilege of getting to know the great Indian leaders of British Columbia. Frank Calder, James Gosnell, and William David McKay top a long list of outstanding leaders and orators. I wanted to be just like them.

I remember that at my first Native Brotherhood meeting an Indian played the piano and everybody stood up to sing "Onward Christian Soldiers." I could not figure this out as Christian religion played no part in my life. I could not see what it had to do with land claims. I was soon to learn some history from my parents and the other Indian leaders.

Under the potlatch laws which were proclaimed in 1884, it was against the law for Indians to gather in numbers of more than three except for family or Christian religious purposes. Attempts by the Indian people to organize for land-claims purposes were specifically outlawed, even to the point of it being illegal for a lawyer to work for Indians.

It must be remembered that the Indian people in British Columbia did not have the provincial vote until 1949 and did not have the federal vote until 1960. This meant that Indians were not citizens and were governed by the archaic rules of the Indian Act.

My father, who was a successful fisherman and businessman, provided well for his large extended family. He also employed many non-Aboriginal people in the Comox Valley. My dad, Charlie Wilson, died in 1959, a year before he could have become a citizen of Canada.

Just as the potlatch went underground so too did political organization for land-claims purposes. The reason the Native Brotherhood of British Columbia began every meeting repeatedly singing a Christian song was because the police officer and the Indian agent would stay at the meeting until they were convinced that it was a Christian gathering and then would leave for their much-needed drink. The Brotherhood meeting would then begin in earnest, with discussion of strategies to pursue land claims.

I repeat this story to illustrate the barriers set up by the non-Aboriginal government through its legislation and legal system, which were designed to prevent the Aboriginal pursuit of freedom. The Indian peoples in British Columbia, particularly the Nisga'a, recognized early on that they must organize themselves to fight for freedom even to the point of going to the newcomers' court.

In 1951 amendments were made to the Indian Act that allowed Indian people to retain lawyers to represent them. As Bev discusses in other parts of this book, a series of court cases was brought forth dealing with land claims, Aboriginal title, and treaty rights. The early landmark decision was Calder et al. v. Attorney General of British Columbia. While a losing decision in the Supreme Court of Canada, it formed the basis of Aboriginal court cases until the 1983 constitutional conference. The 1983 constitutional amendment would become the solid platform on which all future court cases would be built, including the 2014 Xeni Gwet'in (Tsilhqot'in) case.

Let us review. Despite not being regarded as citizens of Canada, Aboriginal people were governed by federal legislation under the Indian Act. Minor relaxation of this archaic legislation allowed Aboriginal people to pursue remedies through the courts, at which point political organization renewed.

It was realized by the Indian leaders, who were subject to the dictates of the Department of Indian Affairs, that the path to their freedom might only be through changing the basic fundamental law by which the government of Canada and the provinces were governed. This meant constitutional change, the opportunity presented by the 1982 patriation.

WHAT IF THE NEWCOMERS AGREE TO NEGOTIATE TERMS OF SETTLEMENT? SHOULD THEY BE ALLOWED TO KEEP CHANGING THE RULES WITHOUT YOUR CONSENT?

1965

Canada Pension Plan excludes Aboriginal people

1977

Canadian Human Rights Act applies everywhere
except on Indian reserves

1985

Bill C-31 restores status to Aboriginal women

Chapter Eight

The Indian Act and Indian Band Governance

MY PERSONAL EXPERIENCE

1980s Onward

EVEN THOUGH substantial amendments had been made to the Indian Act, and even though the 1983 constitutional conference recognized the inherent rights of Aboriginal Canadians, life on the reserve was still a hardship. Aboriginal people continued to fight for change. My community faced ongoing challenges under limitations imposed by the Department of Indian Affairs. They wielded power in all areas of our lives and limited access to housing, wills and estate settlements, as well as financial support for economic development plans. Over the years it became apparent to me that any time someone on the rez wanted to make improvements or do something for themselves, it was almost impossible unless they were strategically positioned to earn their own revenue. For many Indian bands, their remote locations are not ideal. They have to rely on programs designed by the Department of Indian Affairs and other funders. Former chiefs and current chiefs are still trying to change the system. They are the ones in each community who know what works for them. Instead of designing programs that are "one size fits all," individual tribes in the various regions need to be meaningfully involved in how they move forward. Examples of these follow in the form of housing, wills and estates, economic development, and protests that resulted in events such as the Oka Crisis.

BY 1985, A MAJOR change to the Indian Act was underway to address demands for gender equality. The political action to change the act had begun many years before.

In 1970, Jeannette Corbiere Lavell married a non-Native. According to section 12(1)(b) of the Indian Act the following persons are not entitled to be registered: "a woman who married a person who is not an Indian, unless that woman is subsequently the wife or widow of a person described in section 11."

This meant that at that time, an Aboriginal woman who lost her status and her children could no longer live on a reserve. They lost the right to own land or inherit family property. They could not receive treaty benefits or participate in political or social affairs in the community. They even lost the right to be buried in on-reserve cemeteries. However, non-Aboriginal women, even if they were blonde and blue-eyed, were given full rights as Indians if they married Indian men.

Jeannette Corbiere Lavell decided to challenge the Indian Act under the 1960 Bill of Rights. It was the first case dealing with discrimination by reason of sex. In June 1971, Judge Benjamin Grossberg ruled against Jeannette Corbiere Lavell in York County Court. Lavell took it further and on October 9, 1971, the Lavell case was heard in the Federal Court of Appeal, which ruled unanimously for Lavell. The decision was appealed to the Supreme Court of Canada. On August 27, 1973, the Supreme Court, in a majority decision of 5-4, held that the Bill of Rights did not apply to that section of the Indian Act. Lavell lost her case in the Canadian courts.

Years later, Sandra Lovelace, following in Lavell's footsteps, brought the case of status removal to the United Nations International Human Rights Commission, which ruled in her favour.

Finally in April 1985, section 12 of the Indian Act was repealed and Bill C-31, a Bill to Amend the Indian Act, came into effect. Women who had lost their status because of marriage to a non-Aboriginal could apply to be reinstated.

Bill's mom, Ethel Pearson, was a high-ranking matriarch of her nation, the Musgamagw, which means "four people together." Her Musgamagw name, Puugladee, is one of the highest names that can be bestowed in her community. It simply means, "Guests never leave hungry," as Bill says in the foreword to this book. That name in itself says a lot about the culture.

When Ethel married a non-Aboriginal man, she lost her Indian status under the Indian Act. Years later when Bill C-31 came into effect and the women regained their status it was seen as reinstating equality for the women. Ethel, an activist in her own right, was interviewed on a number of occasions and on this particular issue, the reporter asked her, "Mrs. Pearson, what are your thoughts on finally becoming equal?" Ethel shot back at the reporter, "I have *never* been equal in my life and I am not about to take a step down now."

> Ethel shot back at the reporter, "I have *never* been equal in all my life and I am not about to take a step down now."

FURTHER INEQUALITY IS DEMONSTRATED in exclusion of Aboriginal people from the Canada Pension Plan. The CPP, legislated in 1965 and in effect in 1966, is an earnings-related public pension plan that transfers income from workers to the retired. The CPP and its parallel Québec Pension Plan cover all Canadians throughout their working lives – all Canadians, that is, except Aboriginal Canadians.

The government decided that any person working on-reserve would not be allowed to contribute to CPP – or benefit from it. They argued that because Aboriginal people working on reserves don't pay income tax, they should be able to save their money for retirement. And social programs are in place to help those who can't or don't save. The truth is that if you work on-reserve, wages are generally far lower than anywhere else. There are some who can pay their employees good wages but low wages on-reserve are common in most communities.

Then in 2001, Rose Bear challenged the law. Rose Bear asked to make contributions retroactive to 1987 when the Canada Pension Plan was amended to allow voluntary coverage. The federal court judge concluded that the effective exclusion from CPP participation of Indians employed on reserves was discriminatory based on race. The Charter violation could not be justified under section 1. It was further held that the impugned provisions violate the Bill of Rights, paragraph 1(b). Payment of damages was the only claimed relief not granted.

I have worked on a continuous basis since I was sixteen years old. I was a single parent working for very low wages on-reserve and lived from paycheque to paycheque. I applied for employment insurance twice but it did not feed my family. I received one or two cheques before I realized I could not live on that amount. So even though I worked all my life except for when I was in university (with student loans), I did not contribute anything to any type of pension plan. I was forty-eight years old when I went to work for the B.C. Treaty Commission and finally started to pay into a pension plan.

Saving for the future was not an option but, as a young mother of three, retirement was the last thing on my mind. It was only when I was older that I realized the consequences of the situation. Many others who have worked for their Aboriginal communities all of their lives are in the same predicament. They will have to rely only on Old Age Security guaranteed by the federal government. For many non-Native people, to survive on that small income would be a hardship. But the reality is that for many Aboriginal people, it is an increase in monthly income. My mom thought she was the richest person in the world when she started to receive her Old Age Pension of about $1,100 per month. Our community workers now have a pension plan and those who choose to continue to work on-reserve can now be supported during their retirement years.

PASSED IN 1977, the Canadian Human Rights Act applied to all areas of Canada except Indian reserves. Section 67 exempted the Indian Act from provisions of the Canadian Human Rights Act by stating: "Nothing in this Act affects any provision of the Indian Act or any provision made under or pursuant to that Act." That basically ensured that, like the Indian agents had done, the Department of Indian Affairs still made all decisions related to "Indians."

Finally in June 2008, the Canadian Human Rights Act applied to Indian reserves. The 2008 amendment was applied immediately to the federal government but three years later for First Nation governments. The revised legislation meant that First Nation individuals who are registered Indians and members of bands, or individuals residing or working on reserves can make complaints of discrimination to the Canadian Human Rights Commission like anyone else in Canada.

Before 2008 it was pretty much a free-for-all on Indian reserves. Some of the things allowed on-reserve by the federal and provincial governments and later the Aboriginal people in charge have been horrendous. There have been many times in the bad old days when people would just shake their heads at some of the atrocities that were allowed to happen on-reserve. We had nowhere to go with our complaints. Like in the residential schools, we just had to grin and bear it. Since 2008 the federal government and some Indian bands are now being sued for alleged human-rights abuses.

IN MOST COMMUNITIES, the Indian band takes on the mortgage to provide housing for community members. The band needs a ministerial guarantee and in turn has to charge rent for the houses in order to pay the mortgage. Our community has a thirty-five-year mortgage soon to be paid off for houses that were condemned six years after they were built. The funny thing is that even if an individual pays off a mortgage on a house, there is still no guarantee the house will be theirs. There are too many silly rules through the Department of Indian Affairs and the Canadian Mortgage and Housing Corporation (CMHC) that muddy the waters.

My grandmother's house had been built in the 1970s. Every house built the same year has since burned down because of electrical problems. Gram's house, like all the others in the community, was never built to meet any kind of housing code; in fact, there were no standards of any kind for buildings on reserves. The Department of Indian Affairs built my grandmother's house with a budget of a little more than $12,000. That included everything inside the house as well as the septic system and electrical poles needed.

In the 1990s I wanted to renovate the house. Loans on-reserve for anything other than cars are very difficult to get. The only way to secure a loan for a permanent structure such as on-reserve housing is by getting the federal government to basically "co-sign" for you. So under the Indian Act, in order to access monies for housing, you need what is called a ministerial guarantee and that, of course, comes through only with the approval of the Department of Indian Affairs.

Barry Casey, a licensed housing inspector who worked for our tribal council in the early 1990s, helped me do the paperwork and cost estimates for the ministerial guarantee. It turned out I needed $30,000 just to bring the house up to an acceptable standard. After about a month we started to phone the Department of Indian Affairs and badger them about whether or not I was approved for the loan. Barry phoned and I phoned at least every week.

My credit rating at the time was the best one could have. After six months of phoning and badgering the people at the Department of Indian Affairs, I gave up. I was disgusted with the bureaucracy that could not give me an answer. I was sure that it would never be dealt with and what our community called the Black Hole would swallow it up. Like so many things that deal with the Department of Indian Affairs the application for a ministerial guarantee would be lost. Some things, fortunately or unfortunately depending on the circumstances, are never found.

I did not realize it but Barry did not give up and kept up the constant phone calls. After eight months they finally approved the ministerial guarantee. Most people off-reserve would wait a day or two and certainly less than a week to hear from the bank.

I repaid the loan in full. Even though the house could use more renovations I wonder if I have the patience to get another loan. It would need another ministerial guarantee. The bank that we dealt with could not believe the bureaucracy. They said at the time that they would never do another on-reserve loan. It took way too much of their time for a simple $30,000 loan.

Our community has always had problems with housing. The fiscal year for Indian bands is April 1 to March 31. When we first started to administer the funds for housing we would not get any money for housing until October or November, when the ground was frozen. The money, however, had to be spent by the following date of March 31. Anyone who works for an Indian band knows that there are so many restrictive strings attached to any monies we receive. If we do not spend it as the Department of Indian Affairs dictates, then they withhold that amount from our next year's budget. That meant building a house over the cold winter months. Many times trying to dig the frozen ground where a house was to be built was a real challenge. Many homes were faulty because of this and we complained repeatedly to the Department of Indian Affairs asking that we receive the money earlier. Nothing changed.

The first CMHC houses built in our community were supposed to be an improvement; these were the houses condemned within six years. In one house an elderly couple got sick from the poor ventilation and fumes when the furnace was started. In other houses basements flooded, roofs leaked, and in one house water was inside a light fixture in the *basement*. Barry Casey and one of our council members, Dave Pop, did the inspections. Barry wondered how one house did not cave in, the structural foundation was so weak. There was not enough support to hold up the top floor.

Tenants refused to pay the rent because of the poor quality and so it created a lot of bad feelings in the community. We still had to pay the thirty-five-year mortgage and if we didn't the Department of Indian Affairs told us that the money would have to be taken from some of our other programs, such as education. It was tough for council but evictions had to be carried out. There was a long waiting list for people wanting housing and we had to house people who were willing to pay the rent despite the substandard condition of the houses. Unfortunately this scenario has played out many times over the years. It continues to divide the communities.

When we asked the Department of Indian Affairs why the house inspectors did not catch all the deficiencies we were told that they did not provide that type of inspections. They released the money in stages of the completion of the house. For example, money would be released when the foundation had been laid or when the doors and windows were in. They did not inspect to see whether the work was done properly. CMHC did not provide house inspectors at that time either. We were told it was expected the band, through the Department of Indian Affairs, would provide inspectors to ensure the quality of the house. Anyone off-reserve would have walked away from the houses but our community could not. Housing, no matter how bad, was needed and we could not afford to have funding taken from other programs to pay the mortgage. Housing has created a lot of problems for us but we try to deal with the tough situation as best we can.

Before CMHC houses there was a contractor who would come onto the reserve and build houses. The Department of Indian Affairs always hired the same guy. Some of our men in the community, my stepdad being a regular, were invited every now and again to have a drink with him. The contractor always had his stash of booze and built many of the houses in our community, including my grandmother's house that I now occupy. He was incompetent to begin with but the booze made him even more so. On top of that, never did he leave even one piece of wood when he was finished. My stepdad told me that this man built and sold houses outside the reserve with skimmings he took from the building materials that should have been used for houses on the reserve. Many times these "contractors" were blood relations of those in the Department of Indian Affairs who were in charge of approving the contracts.

Another non-Native person who worked for our community had quite a mansion going up. We could see it on our way to the community. He was later fired and as soon as he was fired his house came to a complete stop. I heard he sold it as is and allowed someone else to finish it. Invoices that were later reviewed indicated that certain building materials had never made it to the community. For a long time, it was easy for those looking to take advantage of the community. Today we have more control over the housing in our communities and things have improved, but playing catch-up with housing in Aboriginal communities is still a huge problem. We are looking for ways to fix the problems created by others.

POOR CONSTRUCTION QUALITY created health issues. Lawrence Ogden, my stepdad, died earlier than he should have because of mould in the house he and my mom occupied. Lawrence and my mom were in their mid-seventies and were getting very sick. Lawrence especially was failing. He rarely got out of bed toward the end of his life. After his death we found black mould in his bedroom. The mould was in other parts of the house but caked on the walls of his bedroom. Mom had her own bedroom so was not affected as drastically as Lawrence.

Later the band administration managed to get some money for mould removal and moved Mom out of her house. Mom said that once she moved out of the house temporarily so they could renovate it she started to feel better. She still has lung problems today but some of her health issues disappeared after the removal of the mould. Lawrence was a fatality of the poverty and terrible living conditions that many on reserves have to endure.

ANOTHER LIMITATION IMPOSED on Aboriginal people by bureaucracy in the Department of Indian Affairs was the distribution of wills on-reserve. Twice I was asked to be the executor for estates, once for a non-Aboriginal and once for my former husband. Both estates were quite straightforward, with few assets. When my former husband died, I had acquired a law degree and had already completed one estate for a non-Aboriginal friend. I knew what to do but I could not complete it without the approval of the Department of Indian Affairs. The Department of Indian Affairs has exclusive jurisdiction and authority over the estates of deceased Aboriginals who were registered as an Indian and were ordinarily residents on a reserve before their death. That means that they could, if they saw fit, redistribute the estate. It was a frustrating experience for me at the beginning to know I could not just deal with the will. In the end I did get a very nice lady at the Department of Indian Affairs who was very understanding of my frustration and made the process manageable.

When my grandmother died I knew that she had written a will and so I requested a copy of it. I was there when a fellow from the Department of Indian Affairs visited my grandmother at her home and did her will for her. In response to my request I received a letter that said no such will existed. I settled my grandmother's estate without a will. I knew what she wanted done. About ten years later I received a letter from the Department of Indian Affairs indicating that they recently became aware that my grandmother was deceased and that they were ready to settle the estate. I informed them that I had already taken care of the will years before. They made an issue of it, asking me to provide documents as evidence. I phoned to explain that I had already taken care of it. The person was pretty rude and condescending, an attitude too many in that department have. She informed me that I could not settle the will without their involvement. I was so annoyed and might have thrown a few four-letter words her way. Like so many issues that have to do with the Department of Indian Affairs the will was lost in the Black Hole never to be found again.

When there was a regional office for the Department of Indian Affairs in Prince George we were dealing with an issue for which we had to submit an application. We submitted the application by mail. There was no email in the late 1980s. As chief, I checked a couple of weeks later to see where our application was. They said they had not received it. We did the application again and submitted it, this time by registered mail. A few weeks later I checked again. Once again I was told that they did not have the application. They acknowledged it had come by registered mail but had no idea where it was. The third time I personally drove to Prince George, on my own dime because a travel budget was almost non-existent. I handed it to the person who would be processing the application. I also got him to sign a paper for me acknowledging that he received it from me. We eventually got our funding for the project but not without a lot of work and follow-up on our part. These types of situations happened more times than the Department of Indian Affairs would care to admit.

REMEMBER THE MAN who built a flour mill at Soda Creek? What the Department of Indian Affairs did was charge the man lease fees and that money went into the Soda Creek Indian Band's account in Ottawa. In the late 1980s or early 1990s we had about $60,000 in our revenue account, monies collected from a number of leases on our reserve lands. We decided to invest that money into agriculture and get our fields up and running again. We had a community meeting and everyone was excited and in support of the project.

Times were changing and the older generation who had used horses for haying and transportation were getting too old to work.

The younger generation was not really interested in that style of life. Gone were the days when most of your basic needs could be acquired without money.

Because of this change in lifestyle, younger horses were not bought and the fields fell to ruin. Most of the younger generation worked for minimum wage and so acquiring a tractor and machinery was out of the question. It was not easy to go out and get a loan because the land in newcomer legal terms belonged to the government. And unless the government or someone off-reserve guaranteed a loan there really was no hope of getting a loan to buy machinery. In the early 1970s when the Department of Indian Affairs turned over some of the money to our band council to administer, a few pieces of machinery were purchased. Some families were able to afford the cost of fuel and repairs but for most, it was not within their budgets.

Finally, with the $60,000 in our accounts in Ottawa, we were in a position to get some money up front to get the fields up and running. We worked with a local business in Williams Lake determining what we would need for agriculture, irrigation pipes, and electricity. We did all the paperwork required by the Department of Indian Affairs and sent it off thinking that we could get started soon.

We received a letter from someone in Ottawa who knew nothing about our community. The Department of Indian Affairs decided we couldn't use the money for that particular project because it did not make enough profit. We were not looking to make a profit. We were looking to provide jobs and get the fields up and running again. We tried to argue with them but we were unsuccessful in changing their minds. Today most of the fields still sit in a dilapidated state because the individual people in the community don't have the money up front or the ability to borrow in order to buy machinery. Some programs have achieved limited success like the Special ARDA program (Special Argument and Rural Development Agreement), but for the most part few feasible options are available.

In the early 1970s to the mid-1980s all fifteen Aboriginal communities around Quesnel, 100 Mile House, and Williams Lake formed the Cariboo Tribal Council. There were five Carrier (Alexandria, Nasko, Kluskus, Red Bluff, and Ulkatcho), five Chilcotin (Nemiah, Stone, Anahim, Redstone, and Toosey), and five Secwepemc bands (Soda Creek, Williams Lake, Canoe Creek, Alkali, and Canim Lake). I was not in the chief's position but I attended a number of meetings with Doreen Sellars, my chief at the time. One in particular was held at the old St. Joseph's Mission residential school. All fifteen bands were in attendance. The yearly budgets that each community was going to get were the subject of discussion. The chiefs did not like the budgets that were proposed to them by the Department of Indian Affairs officials. Specifically they did not like the economic development and welfare budgets. The chiefs did not want welfare monies and suggested that the department should give them the same amount they get in welfare but allow them to use it for economic development. The officials from the Department of Indian Affairs told them that they absolutely could not do that. If the chiefs did not accept the welfare money it would simply be sent somewhere else. They were also told that the budgets for economic development would remain the same.

When I was first elected chief of my community in 1987, the economic development monies we received for an entire year totalled approximately $300. (Yes, three hundred dollars!) Our welfare budget, however, was easily more than $100,000. At one point the council and I decided we would make it mandatory for people in the community to work for the welfare monies. There were a lot of things that needed fixing in our community and finding work for people would not have been a problem. We wanted people to be proud of earning their money. Our plan somehow got to the Department of Indian Affairs. We received an official visit from the Indian agent telling me that if we tried to do that, we would be sued. Welfare, we were told, was a right and we could not force people to work for it. Over the years I have watched too many good people get caught in the welfare trap. Thankfully some get out of it but welfare is still ruining people.

Growing up I was always so sensitive to any of the stereotypes of Aboriginal peoples. My grandmother taught me to be clean. Once I got older I was pretty sure I wasn't stupid. Even though I joined in the "party" at times, I stayed away from becoming an alcoholic or drug user. The one stereotype that I avoided like the plague was being on welfare. I have never applied for welfare and have always said I would go live in the bush before going on welfare. There were times when money, no matter how little, would have helped but I absolutely would not ask for help. Because of the training I had received at the residential school I had a hard time asking for help from anyone. The culture of sharing on the rez was strong. We were a small community and everyone pretty well knew everyone's business. I had brothers that hunted and meals were shared willingly with those who needed it.

I SAY THAT some of the machines that take away the work of people should be eliminated. It would be good for the environment and would provide people with jobs. I don't believe anyone wants to be on welfare and I think with a little more thought put into the economy, everyone could contribute just as they did in traditional Aboriginal communities before the newcomers arrived. Obviously there are the disabled and a few others that would need support but most could work for their money and be proud of earning it. There is so much that needs to be done in all of our communities, Native and non-Native alike.

Our community was involved in horse logging for a few years in the late 1980s and early 1990s. We had two Percheron horses. Our community members who worked in the bush loved working with the horses. I went up to our woodlot a few times and was always amazed at how beautiful the area was compared to places where logging was done with only machines. The big machines rip the earth apart and the destruction is extensive. One day two loggers, Lawrence Sellars and Fred Sampson, came into the office at a time of day they would usually be out in the bush. "We have to shut the logging down!" Lawrence said. "Oh no, what happened?" I asked, worrying that something serious had gone wrong. Lawrence had a sly smile and said, "Our skidders are pregnant." We did shut down to allow our horses to have healthy pregnancies. Those few years of horse logging kept a few people employed, made a little bit of money, and did not destroy the earth. Because we were only allowed to log a low percentage of the woodlot, and in response to that along with other changes, the horse logging was abandoned. Too bad it isn't a requirement that more horse logging be done. Those years spent horse logging in the late 1980s and early 1990s were productive for both the land and our people.

IN 1990 A ROADBLOCK between the town of Oka, Quebec, and the Mohawk community of Kanesatake turned into a national crisis. The town of Oka was developing plans to expand a golf course and residential development onto land that was the traditional territory of the Mohawk. The land included a burial ground, marked by standing tombstones of their ancestors. The Mohawks had filed a land claim for the sacred grove and burial ground near Kanesatake but their claim had been rejected in 1986. The rejected claim had not persuaded the Mohawks to abandon their ancestors' final resting place. The result was a seventy-eight-day standoff (July 11 to September 26, 1990) during which the town called in the provincial police, the federal government called in the Canadian military, and Aboriginal people from across Canada threw their support behind the Mohawk. Some travelled to Kanesatake to stand with the Mohawk.

Even though Oka was several thousand kilometres from our area, people in our community felt the tension that was building across the country. One of my cousins went off-reserve to pick up a case of beer. He went into an establishment and ordered a case to take out. He wasn't looking for trouble but the fact that he was Aboriginal was enough for a group of newcomers in the pub. They started harassing him about Oka and beat him up. When this young man finally was able to leave, he went to the rez, picked up a number of other young guys, and went back to the pub to finish the fight. Incidents like this were common in Canada during what they called the Oka Crisis. I believe it was the Mohawk who were the ones in crisis because they were trying to protect the resting place of their ancestors.

Oka established a broader awareness of Native grievances that had long simmered away from public attention. Even though there were other protests, this one was observed in many parts of the world, as was another one quite close to home in the Cariboo near Soda Creek. The Gustafsen Lake Standoff took place near 100 Mile House, a community not far from Soda Creek, in the summer of 1995. For more than thirty days, Royal Canadian Mounted Police stood off against sundancers at a camp outside of town. Even though it is a significant historic moment that happened in our territory I only knew what the rest of the people knew via television. I was in Victoria doing my undergrad at the time. I was not involved with leadership and so do not feel comfortable speaking to this particular standoff. Others can speak to it more knowledgably.

Aboriginal people in Canada along with indigenous people around the world are more determined than ever to have our issues dealt with. In the communication age we live in today, it is no longer possible to keep Aboriginal issues out of sight and out of mind. More and more newcomers are now learning about the tremendous injustices that Aboriginal people in all the Americas have endured. For example, a report by the Environics Institute for Survey Research released in June 2016 found that a growing percentage of non-aboriginal Canadians believe Aboriginal people experience regular discrimination that's comparable to or worse than that faced by other minorities.

THE INDIAN ACT SETS UP what it calls "band councils" so that all the reporting is done to funding agencies. When I was chief there was absolutely no requirement for me to report to the individuals in the community. I could have gone through my twelve years as chief without consulting with them. But the amount of reporting we did to the Department of Indian Affairs and other funding agencies was unreal.

In her 2002 report Canada's auditor general, Sheila Fraser, estimated that each Indian reserve was required to file 168 reports annually to just the top four federal organizations receiving their reports. In 2011 she reported, "Despite many initiatives, we have not seen a significant reduction in the reporting burden."

Fraser found that "it remains unclear whether this degree of reporting helps make First Nations accountable, or whether it assists either the Department or First Nations with their management responsibilities," adding that "some of these reports may serve little purpose and may interfere with First Nations' ability to meet the needs of their members."

In a November 2012 report, the government confirmed what the auditor general had been saying. The deputy minister reported, "First Nations and other organizations that receive funding from the Government of Canada are caught in a complex web of reporting requirements, some of which are of dubious usefulness to them or to the organizations seeking the reports." These statements illustrate that Aboriginal people are still held back by rules and regulations that would not be acceptable anywhere else.

WHAT IF YOU ARE FORCED TO APPEAL TO NEWCOMER INSTITUTIONS AND LAWS TO TRY TO GET YOUR HOUSE BACK? DOES THAT JUSTIFY LEGAL TRANSFER OF THE HOUSE TO THEM WITHOUT YOUR CONSENT?

1998

Delgamuukw decision determines Aboriginal land title had never been extinguished

2000

Nisga'a agreement signed as the first modern-day treaty in British Columbia

2014

Xeni Gwet'in decision grants the right of Aboriginal bands to decide how territorial land will be used

Chapter Nine

Re-establishing Aboriginal Rights

SUPREME COURT OF CANADA DECISIONS FROM CALDER TO TSILHQOT'IN

1973 to 2015

IF YOU OWNED a house and you invited others who needed a place to stay to come and stay in your house, is it still your house? What if you got sick and members of your family died, and the ones you initially welcomed invited more of their own to come and live in your house – even though they now outnumber your family – does it make the house theirs? What if your rules for the house are ignored and the newcomers impose their own rules in the house, does ownership of the house transfer? And if eventually you are displaced to the garage and the newcomers use up the best part of the house, does that make the house theirs? To try to get your rights and title to the house acknowledged you are forced to go into their foreign institution and the laws you are forced to argue are all theirs, but does that justify legally transferring the house to them without your consent?

These questions call up an understanding of basic property rights, but they also apply to the fight within the Canadian court system to re-establish Aboriginal rights and title. The newcomers came to visit and then decided to make the house their own. The house has many rooms, though, enough for all to live comfortably – as long as everyone's rights are respected, especially those of the original owners.

WHILE ABORIGINAL ORGANIZATIONS were struggling to establish themselves and gain recognition in the political arena they were also fighting battles of equal significance in the courts. Aboriginal people knew without a doubt that their title was never extinguished. Finally there was some progress for Aboriginal peoples.

Long before Aboriginal people were able to use the Canadian courts to advance their grievances there had been Canadian legal precedents set. The very foundation of Aboriginal ownership of lands was recognized in the Royal Proclamation of King George III, October 7, 1763, who acknowledged the Aboriginal right to possess, occupy, and use the territory.

St. Catherine's Milling and Lumber Co. v. the Queen, decided in 1888, was a court case that for years prevailed as the dominant case for Aboriginal title, until the Calder decision in 1973. In St. Catherine's Milling, the court ruled that title was a usufructuary right for Aboriginal people; in other words, title and that right existed at the pleasure of the Crown. The St. Catherine's Milling decision claimed that Aboriginal title was granted by the Crown through the Royal Proclamation. Even though this court case acknowledges Aboriginal title, it is the Aboriginal people's view that you cannot grant someone something that is already theirs.

There are many ground-breaking legal cases that Aboriginal people have won since legal representation was allowed and the ban on the pursuit of land claims was lifted in the 1951 amendments to the Indian Act. This chapter covers only a few cases and each case is discussed in overview. All of the cases involve so much more than I will highlight but the intent for this book is just to give a quick glimpse into each of the major court cases. These cases worked their way through the lower courts but eventually made it to the Supreme Court of Canada, the highest court in Canada, because each merited evaluation of a new principle of law or established a test for the consideration of future cases with similar legal principles.

IN 1973, THE Supreme Court of Canada ruled in Calder, a court action brought by the Nisga'a nation against the Attorney General of British Columbia. The Nisga'a sought a declaration "that the aboriginal title, otherwise known as Indian title, of the Plaintiffs to their ancient tribal territory ... has never been lawfully extinguished." The Nisga'a lost at trial and at the Court of Appeal but the Supreme Court of Canada ruled that the Nisga'a held title to their land before settlers came; three justices ruled that Nisga'a title still exists today, three said it was extinguished when British Columbia joined Canada and one refused to rule either way. The case was dismissed on a technicality because under British Columbia law, an action could not be taken against the government without a fiat conferring prior permission to sue the Crown. Although many were disappointed, the Nisga'a and other Aboriginal people considered it a victory. For the first time in history, even though it was a foreign law system for the Aboriginal peoples, three Supreme Court of Canada judges said Nisga'a title still existed. The issue of whether the Nisga'a held title to the land before the newcomers came is ludicrous. Of course they did.

> Before the court case Frank Calder, a Nisga'a leader in the video *This Land* stated, "The Nisga'a Tribal Council isn't on trial. The Nass River people are not on trial in this issue. The Indians in British Columbia are not on trial. *British justice* is on trial. "

Before the court case Frank Calder, a Nisga'a leader in the video *This Land* stated, "The Nisga'a Tribal Council isn't on trial. The Nass River people are not on trial in this issue. The Indians in

British Columbia are not on trial. *British justice* is on trial. British justice is on trial."

Frank Howard (NDP-Skeena) introduced a bill in the House of Commons hours after the Calder decision was handed down, requiring Parliament to recognize the Aboriginal titles of Native peoples in British Columbia. The Bill would authorize the government to negotiate Native land claims, including the question of any compensation to be paid for extinguishing these claims. Howard was unable to start a debate in the House on the issue of Aboriginal rights, but the justice minister at the time, Otto Lang, said he would have an early discussion with Indian Affairs Minister Jean Chrétien and recommend a number of alternatives to deal with the "problem" posed by the decision. Until 1991 when the British Columbia Task Force, which was made up of representatives from the federal, provincial, and Aboriginal governments set up the B.C. Treaty Process, the Nisga'a were the only ones in British Columbia at the negotiating table.

After years of continually fighting for their title and rights, on May 11, 2000, the Nisga'a Final Agreement was signed. In their brochures for the Final Agreement the Nisga'a wrote, "Some were young when they joined the cause but grew old seeking an agreement that would benefit future generations." Every Aboriginal nation can say the same thing about their people who continue to fight for the future of their grandchildren.

THE GUERIN DECISION in 1985 confirmed that the federal government must protect the interests of Aboriginal people. It also recognized that Aboriginal rights existed before Canada became a country and that those rights apply both on- and off-reserve. The facts of the case were that the Musqueam Indian Band in the Vancouver area had surrendered valuable lands to the government for lease to put in a golf club. The lease monies, however, were much less than those approved by Musqueam at the surrender meeting. The Musqueam did not get the information about the terms of lease until many years later. The Supreme Court of Canada decision in Guerin provided one of the most important decisions regarding the Crown's fiduciary relationship with Aboriginal people. Based on this case, the federal government was being sued right, left, and centre.

THE SUPREME COURT of Canada decision in a fisheries case called Sparrow in 1990 established standards of conduct for both the federal and provincial governments and clarified the fiduciary responsibility of the federal government with regard to Aboriginal rights. The SCC ruled that section 35 of the Constitution Act, 1982, provides "a strong measure of protection" for Aboriginal rights; it further ruled that Aboriginal and treaty rights are capable of evolving over time and must be interpreted in a generous and liberal manner.

The Court's ruling resulted in what is known today as the "Sparrow test," which sets out a list of criteria that determines whether a right is existing, and if so, how a government may be justified to infringe upon it.

Although many recognize the Sparrow case as a significant victory for those interested in the affirmation of Aboriginal rights, the courts also said that these rights are not absolute and can be infringed upon providing the government can legally justify it. Further, the Court did not outline what would qualify as adequate consultation or compensation regarding rights infringement. Van der Peet, decided by the Supreme Court of Canada in 1996, further defined Aboriginal rights as outlined in Section 35 of the Constitution Act, 1982. Van der Peet's right to fish goes beyond Sparrow to further define a test for distinctive cultural use of the fishery. Outstanding questions regarding adequate consultation with First Nations would eventually be examined in the Supreme Court decisions Taku River Tlingit (2004) and Haida Nation (2004).

THE GITXSAN AND WET'SUWET'EN sought recognition of their Aboriginal title in northwestern British Columbia. In 1997 the Supreme Court of Canada did not rule on the specifics of the

Gitxsan-Wet'suwet'en case but it said some very important things. Delgamuukw v. British Columbia (Attorney General) (1997) had concerned the definition, the content, and the extent of Aboriginal title.

The Supreme Court said that Aboriginal title constituted an ancestral right protected by section 35(1) of the Constitution Act, 1982. Aboriginal title is *sui generis* and so distinguished from other proprietary rights. Aboriginal title is, therefore, in substance, a right to territory and encompasses exclusive use and occupation. It is inalienable and cannot be transferred, sold, or surrendered to anyone other than the Crown.

The Court determined that in order for Aboriginal people to prove existence of Aboriginal title the following requirements needed to be in place: "(i) they must have occupied the territory before the declaration of sovereignty; (ii) if present occupation is invoked as evidence of occupation before sovereignty, there must be a continuity between present occupation and occupation before the declaration of sovereignty; (iii) at the time of declaration of sovereignty, this occupation must have been exclusive." It is not necessary to prove a perfect continuity; the demonstration of a substantial maintenance of the bond between the people concerned and the territory is sufficient.

Before this court case, oral history was not admissible because the courts said it was "hearsay." That basically left all of the oral history that had been passed down for generations unusable. Quite ironic I would suggest: the written word, however inaccurate, could be accepted but not oral history. The rules these foreign courts make up are sometimes downright silly. This court case, however, determined that oral evidence could be admitted as proof.

The court also ruled that Aboriginal lands could not be used in a manner that was inconsistent with Aboriginal title: if Aboriginals wished to use the lands in ways that Aboriginal title did not permit, then the lands must be surrendered. Aboriginal title cannot be transferred to anyone other than the Crown. Court cases still, without the consent of the Aboriginal people, make rules that

Aboriginal people may very well disagree with. I am not saying I disagree with this; I am saying that law such as this will continue to restrict Aboriginal people by letting others dictate what we can and cannot do with our lands. That should be an individual nation decision, not an imposed foreign court decision.

Aboriginal title is a right to the land itself but these court cases did not clarify how and where Aboriginal title exists. The courts encouraged the parties to negotiate to settle these questions.

ON JUNE 26, 2014, the Supreme Court of Canada issued a historic ruling of Aboriginal title to the Tsilhqot'in people. The Supreme Court of Canada released a unanimous 8-0 decision acknowledging the truth of what the Xeni Gwet'in peoples of the Tsilhqot'in Nation have always known: they have title to their traditional territory in the Chilcotin area. Granted it is not all that they wanted the court to acknowledge but it is a good start for solid negotiations.

The court held that "a declaration of Aboriginal title over the area requested should be granted. A declaration that British Columbia breached its duty to consult is owed to the Tsilhqot'in Nation and should also be granted."

Building on the ground-breaking ruling by Justice David Vickers in 2007, the Supreme Court of Canada granted Aboriginal title to 1,750 square kilometres, thereby firmly and finally denying the narrow view of title that was under appeal. The Supreme Court ruled that "occupation sufficient to ground Aboriginal title is not confined to specific sites of settlement but extends to tracts of land that were regularly used for hunting, fishing or otherwise exploiting resources and over which the group exercised effective control at the time of assertion of European sovereignty." This ruling marks the first time the Supreme Court has recognized Aboriginal title to a specific lot of land.

This ruling of Aboriginal title confers several rights: the right to decide how the land will be used; the right to economic benefit from the land; and the right to proactively use and manage the land.

The court said, "The right to control the land conferred by Aboriginal title means that governments and others seeking to use the land must obtain the consent of the Aboriginal title holders." If consent is not provided, "the government's only recourse is to establish that the proposed incursion on the land is justified under s.35 of the Constitution Act, 1982."

The Supreme Court of Canada found that the B.C. Forest Act does not apply to the Tsilhqot'in Aboriginal title lands; in fact, the beneficial interest in the land, including its resources, belongs to the Tsilhqot'in title holders.

Of course, just as in all the other wins in the Supreme Court of Canada, the Aboriginal people celebrated while the government lawyers continue to find ways to limit what Aboriginal people can demand in relation to their land. The struggle continues.

In 2012 treaty rights negotiator Bill Gallagher, commenting on the rise of Native empowerment in Canada's resources sector, observed that Aboriginal people had won more than 150 court cases to date. The 2014 case of Tsilhqot'in Nation v. British Columbia added significantly to this legal winning streak and marked a major milestone in Aboriginal resistance to the effects of colonization.

SO WHAT DO these and other court cases mean according to the non-Aboriginal courts of law? They mean that Aboriginal rights exist in Canadian law and are distinct and different from the rights of other Canadians. They mean that the legal and constitutional status of Aboriginal people derives from the fact they are the descendants of the peoples and governing societies that resided in North America long before the newcomers arrived. They mean that Aboriginal rights and title are solidified in the Canadian government structure and cannot be extinguished because the Constitution Act, 1982, protects them. They mean that government has a duty to consult and possibly accommodate Aboriginal interests even where title has not been proven. And they mean a lot more – but that is beyond the scope of this book.

It is important to recognize that our struggles for justice since the newcomers arrived have not been fought alone. Aboriginal people have had the support right from the beginning of some who saw the injustice of it all. The many court cases each cost millions of dollars. Many Aboriginal communities are the poorest of the poor in Canada and could never have done it alone. Funds were raised in any way the Aboriginal people could bring in money. This would include bingos, bake sales, bannock sales, and many other fundraising efforts. Thankfully there are also non-Aboriginal groups that exist specifically to help Aboriginal people move their causes forward.

THE MOST RECENT court win for Aboriginal people, the 2014 Xeni Gwet'en case, takes us the closest to how Aboriginal people view their territories. It is not a total win but a victory that Aboriginal leaders in the province of British Columbia have struggled to achieve. Now resource development must include informed consent of the Aboriginal people in their territories.

The early Aboriginal groups such as the Allied Indian Tribes of British Columbia and the Native Brotherhood of British Columbia must certainly be credited with the initiatives that kept this struggle alive. As Bill says, "Land claims, land claims, land claims" was always their mantra. Despite the fact that these organizations have basically disappeared, their vision has helped shift the balance of power back to the Aboriginal people.

Aboriginal people faced with resource development initiatives now have the big stick in their hands. They not only have to be consulted properly, they very likely have to approve major development projects on their land before they proceed. We have not arrived at the right of refusal but some believe we are close. Future court cases may very well establish the Aboriginal peoples' right to say no to activities not in their interest.

While the precise content of title and rights for both the Crown and Aboriginal people is not yet agreed upon, documents which started with the Royal Proclamation, followed by court cases and the Canadian constitution, provide a solid legal base upon which Aboriginal people can move forward. The irony in all of this is that the federal government is supposed to be looking after the best interests of the "Indians" and yet they have been our biggest opponent at every turn. The governments continues to spend millions, probably billions over the years, of taxpayers' money to try to deny our human rights. I have heard that the majority of lawyers working for the federal government are assigned to deal with Aboriginal matters. Whether this is true or not, it certainly does employ many, many lawyers to work on Aboriginal issues.

THE GOVERNMENT IS now desperately trying to get out of its fiduciary duty through many avenues, modern-day treaties being one option. Between 1923 and 1973, no new treaties were signed. This started to change when the Nisga'a Tribal Council launched a legal action in 1968. It ended with the Supreme Court of Canada's 1973 decision in the Calder case, which as we have seen forced the federal government to develop a policy to address Aboriginal land issues across Canada. This became known as the Comprehensive Claims Policy, dealing with areas of Canada where Aboriginal people's claims to Aboriginal rights have not been addressed by treaties or other legal means. The first of these modern-day treaties was the James Bay and Northern Quebec Agreement, signed in 1975. Since 1973, several treaties have been negotiated and signed:

James Bay and Northern Quebec Agreement (1975) – Quebec
Northeastern Quebec Agreement (1978) – Quebec
Inuvialuit Final Agreement (1984) – Northwest Territories
Gwich'in Comprehensive Land Claim Agreement (1992) –
    Northwest Territories
Tungavik Federation of Nunavut Comprehensive Claim
    Agreement (1993) – Northwest Territories
Sahtu Dene and Metis Comprehensive Land Claim
    Agreement (1994) – Northwest Territories

Vuntut Gwitchin First Nation Final Agreement
(1994) – Yukon

First Nation of Na-cho Ny'a'k Dun Final Agreement
(1994) – Yukon

Teslin Tlingit Council Final Agreement (1994) – Yukon

Champagne and Aishihik First Nations Final Agreement
(1994) – Yukon

Little Salmon/Carmacks First Nations Final Agreement
(1997) – Yukon

Selkirk First Nation Final Agreement (1997) – Yukon

VTr'ondëk Hwech'in First Nation Final Agreement
(1998) – Yukon

Tsawwassen First Nation Final Agreement (2007) – British
Columbia

Maa-nulth First Nation Final Agreement (2010)
– British Columbia

These modern treaties deal with issues related to lands and resources. Some provide for the negotiation of self-government agreements as well.

Until the negotiation of the Nisga'a Final Agreement the only treaties affecting the province of British Columbia were Treaty 8, which in 1899 was extended from Alberta into northeastern British Columbia, and the fourteen treaties on Vancouver Island that Governor James Douglas negotiated between 1850 and 1854.

TREATY NEGOTIATIONS HAVE required incredible strength on the part of Aboriginal leaders. This reminds me of a story Bill told me about a time former Musqueam Chief Ernie Campbell instructed him to meet with government representatives about treaty issues. Ernie insisted that compensation be on the table and insisted that Bill be the one to meet with negotiators. The federal government had previously said no to compensation. In order to introduce compensation as a discussion item, Bill arrived early and alone at the Federal Treaty Negotiation office and took his place at the negotiation table.

Already seated were eight to ten provincial representatives and at least sixteen federal representatives, most of them lawyers. The federal treaty negotiation officer chairing the meeting looked at Bill sitting alone at one end of the table and asked him if he was expecting anyone else to represent the Indian cause. When Bill said no, the federal guy said, "This meeting looks a bit unbalanced and perhaps unfair." Bill said, "Well if you want to go for more help I am more than willing to wait for you."

> Bill said, "Well if you want to go for more help I am more than willing to wait for you."

Treaty settlements in all parts of Canada, successful court cases by Aboriginal people, and the growing support of public opinion helped change British Columbia's stance on negotiating with Aboriginal people. In 1991 the provincial government joined Canada at the negotiating table by establishing the B.C. Treaty Commission to resolve the land question in British Columbia. Uncertainty was not something the governments and industry wanted to deal with on a regular basis.

A task force made up of representatives from the federal, provincial, and Aboriginal governments formed to set up a treaty process. The task force released a report in 1991 with nineteen recommendations on how treaties should be negotiated and a six-stage treaty process that established criteria for entering treaty negotiations. Aboriginal people were no longer required, as the Nisga'a had been, to provide detailed information and evidence concerning use and occupancy of their traditional lands. No longer would Aboriginal people need to *prove*, as the Nisga'a were required to do, that they were here and using the land before the newcomers came.

Aboriginal groups are required to borrow money from the federal and provincial governments to be at the negotiating table. The funding is broken down approximately as 80 percent loan and 20 percent grants. When I left my position as chief in 2015, my tribal council had borrowed more than $22 million to negotiate treaties.

This debt sits on our books as an accounts payable item, and the banks do not like to loan money to organizations burdened with that kind of financial obligation. Add this to the fact that banks do not like to loan money on-reserve and this debt makes it very difficult for some communities. The B.C. Treaty Commission is in charge of making sure the Aboriginal peoples spend the money as they should. None of the money is to be used for legal challenges. As soon as there is any legal challenge, the negotiations are shut down by the governments. The money Aboriginal groups can borrow also stops. This is crazy because as someone once said, "Negotiations are usually concluded on the courthouse steps when they cannot agree. Someone threatens to take the other side to court." Aboriginal groups do not have that option.

Even though a few nations have managed to conclude a treaty with the governments, the treaty process for most nations have ended up in the same way as the Indian Act: if something does not suit the governments, they go back and change the rules. First Nations were eager to finally get to the table thinking they would be negotiating on equal footing. Instead we were told that the negotiations were not "rights" based so it didn't matter how many court cases we had won. And yet we are continually reminded by the government that the non-Aboriginal

> When I left my position as chief in 2015, my tribal council had borrowed more than $22 million to negotiate.

"rights" to the land that currently exist have to be considered. The governments do not want to have to pay compensation to those rights holders but we are told that they will not pay past compensation for our rights. We were also told, "No, we don't want to talk about fish. No, we don't want to talk about self-government as Aboriginal people see it. No, no, no, no, no ..."

Some treaty settlement lands being offered are smaller than other existing reserves. Take the Osoyoos Indian Reserve as an example. The reserve spans 32,000 acres with 520 community members. Osoyoos has done very well for itself and I applaud them. My point is that our community is comparable in membership and yet the offer we got from the governments was nowhere near what Osoyoos has had since 1877. Other reserves in Alberta are absolutely huge. On top of that some small Aboriginal communities have borrowed more money to negotiate than they could ever hope to get in a treaty settlement.

ON NOVEMBER 12, 2010, the Canadian government endorsed the United Nations Declaration on the Rights of Indigenous Peoples. Several days later the First Nations Summit issued a joint statement in response urging the government to move ahead with the implementation of its provisions "in a principled manner that fully respects [Aboriginal peoples'] spirit and intent." The Summit statement went on to describe the declaration as "more than an aspirational instrument," but as a document to assist with interpretation of the human rights of Aboriginal people and government obligations for them. The declaration establishes minimum standards for the survival, dignity, security, and well-being of indigenous peoples.

The declaration's provisions reflect established international human rights standards, including those that are already legally binding because they are part of general and customary international law. It is simply inaccurate for the government to continue to claim that the declaration "does not reflect customary international law." This is a "manifestly untenable position" as concluded by the UN Special Rapporteur on the rights of indigenous peoples in his 2014 report on Canada.

Canada was one of only four countries to vote against the declaration when it was adopted by the UN General Assembly on September 13, 2007. In the last three years, the government aggressively campaigned against the declaration, opposing its use. Both domestically and in international fora, the government has attempted to undermine the specific rights and related state obligations in this human rights instrument. Such ongoing actions are affecting present and future generations in international negotiations on biodiversity, climate change, and intellectual property.

"We remain concerned that Canada's actions, both domestically and abroad, are not reflecting the standards that the government now professes to support," said Grand Chief Edward John of the First Nations Summit. In May 2016 Canada officially removed itself as an objector to the declaration. Canada's Minister of Indigenous Affairs told the United Nations in New York, "Canada is now a full supporter of the [UN Declaration on the Rights of Indigenous Peoples] without qualification." Still, as Grand Chief Edward John said some years ago, "Actions are more important than words. We will be looking for concrete evidence that the government's endorsement of the declaration reflects a genuine willingness to uphold its provisions."

THE DECLARATION SAYS, among other things, that Aboriginal people have the right to "free, prior, and informed consent" over development on their traditional land. Perry Bellegarde, national chief of the Assembly of First Nations (AFN), pointed out in a May 2016 statement to the UN Permanent Forum on Indigenous Issues in New York that this duty to consult is non-binding: the word *veto* does not appear in either the declaration or in the 2014 Tsilhqot'in decision where the Supreme Court of Canada said the government must seek the consent of Aboriginal communities when it intends to interfere in lands to which they have title, unless it can make a strong case that the infringement is in the public good." Bellegarde went on to say that "obtaining the consent of affected indigenous groups before starting a resource project is now considered a best practice." One such group is the Secretariat of the Boreal Leadership Council – a collection of conservation groups, First Nations, resource companies, and financial institutions with stakes in Canada's boreal forest – Alan Young, director of the secretariat said: "It's how you avoid delays. It's how you build lasting stable relationships. That is the view of many leaders now and it's welcome that the government has caught up." I can only recommend the same practice. It is because of the destruction of our territories that we continue to fight for a say in what happens there.

ON AUGUST 4, 2014, I was about to leave Vancouver on my way back to my home community when I saw on Facebook images of the tailings pond breach that had occurred at the Mount Polley copper and gold mine, a subsidiary of Imperial Metals and Energy. It was later determined that, when the Mount Polley tailings dam failed, it sent seventeen million cubic metres of water and eight million cubic metres of waste materials into Polley Lake, Hazeltine Creek, and Quesnel Lake. The mine is in Secwepemc territory that our community shares with the Williams Lake Indian Band. Quesnel Lake is an important place for our people. It is a rainforest in the middle of the province where our people go to collect medicinal plants not available in other parts of our territory. I thought the Facebook posts were some sort of joke until I received a call from Councillor Willie Sellars from the Williams Lake Indian Band asking me if I had seen the news. He confirmed that this was not a joke. Like so many others, I was in shock. I told Bill as I was leaving his apartment, "It is going to be a long month!" Little did I know that a month would turn into years and still our communities continue to fight to have the government and the mine be held accountable for their actions.

There is no good time for a mine breach such as this but it was the worst possible time because the annual salmon runs were on their way up the Fraser River. Quesnel Lake flows into the Quesnel River, which flows into the Fraser River. Water tests showed elevated levels of selenium, arsenic, and other metals in the water near the breach. At a community meeting organized for the day following the breach, I heard elders and community members express their pain and fear about the Mount Polley disaster. It was intense with lots of tears. People were scared of eating the fish and many freezers were left empty that winter. I have not harvested salmon from the Fraser River for approximately fifteen years now. I am not the only one. Our people tried to warn the federal Department of Fisheries and Oceans about thirty years ago about the changes we saw in the salmon. They tried to convince us those changes were normal. The cancer rates in our community are extremely high. People are looking at the fish as one possible cause.

The Fraser River has been on the endangered list for many years. Owners of pulp mills, mines, and other resource companies think nothing of discharging their pollutants into the river. As long as they make money, to heck with the environment and the rights of those who depend on the resources that swim in the river and grow or walk on the land. The future predicted in the Cree proverb is approaching: "Only when the last tree has died and the last river been poisoned and the last fish been caught will we realize we cannot eat money." It also reminds me of a chief I met in Ecuador who said that the mines came in and offered their community a lot of money. Because the mine would have drastically harmed their environment, the chief told them, "You can eat your money soup. We will eat our banana soup and we will see who survives."

The Aboriginal relationship to the land is spiritual. Many know that Mother Earth is alive and everything has a soul. In the Secwepemc culture, a woman often is given a name that ends in a word that refers to water. Water is life-giving and so too are women, explains Secwepemc elder Cecilia DeRose. Disrespecting and losing land is like, for Aboriginal peoples, cutting off a part of who we are. As Indian Reserve Commissioner Gilbert Sproat wrote in a letter to the superintendent of Indian Affairs in April 1879: "I do not exaggerate in saying that some of these Indians die if they lose their land: they take it so much to heart." So when Mount Polley breached, that is what the community was feeling.

I GREW UP ON the banks of the Fraser River and the annual salmon run was a time of great excitement. Canning jars were washed, smoke houses were fixed up, and the specialized wood for smoking was gathered. Everyone kept an ear to the ground about the first fish coming up the river. The moccasin telegraph was pretty accurate and so we knew where the fish were at most times and how many days it would take them to get to us.

When the fish did arrive, the first fish caught was cut up in ceremonial fashion and thrown into a pot of boiling water. The fresh fish that had travelled hundreds of kilometres up the Fraser River to our village always tasted so good. Fishing season was *the* summer social event and even if you weren't fishing, the river was the place to be. Fishing happened almost always at night because the canyons where we fished were too hot during the day. The fish would have gone bad quickly. People would pack their flashlight, sacks, and net, and head to the river. It was magical looking up and down the river and seeing the many campfires where others were fishing.

If the fish were not running in great numbers, people would wander around on the well-worn trails to other fishing sites to visit and share a coffee. I loved being down the river during fishing season and was pretty much a river rat during my teens until my mid-thirties. I remember standing at a fishing spot one night with my cousin Bernice, who was just a few years older than me. We were counting the number of fires on the river and sharing information about who was fishing at each site. She said, "Someone should write a song about this; it is not going to last." I was really upset with her for saying that. I couldn't imagine how it could change let alone disappear altogether. Obviously she saw something that I didn't.

When I first started fishing the river with my older relatives, the fish arrived like clockwork. On my sister, Teena's birthday, July 15, salmon season was in full swing. The fish were silver, strong, and when they were thrown out of the net into the fish pit, they put up a good fight to get back into the river, flopping around trying to get out. We had to club their heads to quiet them down.

About thirty years ago we started to see the changes in the fish. At first we noticed scars on them, parts of their heads would be cut, or the sides of their bodies marked. Then we started to see worms in the fish. The fish were almost dead; they hardly struggled to get back in the river. And we could no longer tell when they were going to come up the river. All of this was alarming and we reported it to officers of the federal Department of Fisheries and Oceans. "Oh that's normal," they said and dismissed our concerns, but not before one DFO officer warned us not to eat the salmon eggs anymore. He said they had a high concentration of a heavy metal. The salmon eggs were a delicacy to many of our people but I have not eaten salmon eggs since then. The changes we were seeing in the fish were not normal.

Even though I noticed disturbing changes over the years, I continued to harvest fish every year until one year when my brother brought me a tub of fish. I started cutting them up to hang in the smokehouse. There were so many worms in them that I quit cutting. I opened a few other fish and they were the same. For the first time in my life, I allowed salmon to go to waste and refused to process them. I have not fished on the Fraser River or eaten any of the fish in about fifteen years. My smokehouse is now used as a toolshed.

My children inherited harvesting rights from their dad in the Nuxalk territory (Bella Coola). Fish is no longer a regular part of my diet but the small amount of fish I get comes from there. The saddest part of all of this is the knowledge that along with the loss of the fish will be the loss of part of our culture. My grandchildren will never know the joy of traditional fishing on the Fraser River. My grandson has been going to Bella Coola with his mom for years and has learned how to process fish Nuxalk-style. My daughter, Jacinda, also took her nieces, Mya and Kiara, ages thirteen and eleven at the time, down last year and they participated for the first time in learning to process Nuxalk-style.

We are also seeing changes in the wildlife in our area. A few years ago my son Scott shot a moose and I asked him to bring me the liver and heart. If anyone has ever seen a moose liver you will know that they are huge, at least a couple of feet long. Scott came in with a shrivelled-up piece of something that fit into his cupped hands. He said, "Mom, I think this is the liver." Turned out it was a very damaged liver. We were shocked and concerned. Others in our community have noticed unhealthy organs in animals.

My sister, Teena, shot a moose and had to leave it in the bush. It was the first time she had ever encountered anything like that even though she had hunted with her dad since she was very young. The moose was sick and full of open sores of some sort. When we reported these things, we never heard back or Fish and Wildlife officers brushed it off as normal or an isolated case. Thankfully that is changing and government workers are now involving Aboriginal people in some areas.

I have always said that Aboriginal people see the changes on the land first because we gather our food and medicines from it. Governments need to incorporate this knowledge into the monetary economy that drives the country otherwise the monetary economy will kill the natural economy. We are all in trouble then.

People say there are only two things in life that are certain: death and taxes. I always say that there is a third thing that is also certain, the fact that Aboriginal people will always be in their homelands. The Indian problem for some non-Aboriginal people, as defined by my daughter, Jacinda, "is that we are still here." The reality is that we will always be here. And, for the record *we are not nomadic people*. Our Mother Country and our Holy Lands have been and always will be here in the Americas. We will always be here fighting for our rights and the environment as our ancestors did.

The governments need to realize that resource extraction will not be a "quick and easy" solution to add to the short-term economy. The resource extraction economy needs to be totally re-evaluated to protect the environment. Maybe the mines should be mining in the garbage dumps before going to pristine areas. We individually have a responsibility to change this as well. As long as we keep buying useless junk that fills the dumps, we too are as guilty as the big companies and governments.

Another example is gold. There is no need to mine any more gold. Fifty to 80 percent of gold goes to make jewellery, so for the vanity of those who can afford it, the environment is destroyed. The short-term jobs gold mining provides can in no way compare to the destructive long-term effects on the environment. When it comes to resource extraction, Aboriginal people are always criticized for stopping employment. What others need to realize is that we are not just fighting for our grandchildren – we are fighting for everyone's grandchildren. It is our absolute duty to speak for those who cannot yet speak for themselves. It is our absolute duty to speak for those that do not have a voice. *Change is never easily accepted.* That is the David-and-Goliath fight for us all. Thankfully many non-Aboriginals have joined the fight to protect "all our relations." I have been told on a number of occasions by non-Aboriginal people who either live off the land or know the importance of a healthy eco-system that they are looking to the Aboriginal people to protect it. They know we have more of a voice when it comes to dealing with government. Unfortunately as it exists now, unless governments are hit with a court decision, the resource-extraction companies have a powerful voice as well.

A GREAT EXAMPLE of how governments can work with Aboriginal people is found in Haida Gwaii off the west coast of British Columbia. Haida Gwaii is a series of islands split between north and south. The southern part is known is Gwaii Haanas National Park Reserve and Haida Heritage Site and is protected through the Archipelago Management Board, the co-operative management body made up of representatives of the Government of Canada and the Council of the Haida Nation. In the north is Graham Island where the majority of the Haida and non-Haida population reside.

The Haida people fought to keep their lands from being destroyed through stand-offs, and the major one that attracted media attention was the Lyell Island confrontation in 1985.

Haida Gwaii is an example of how two groups with differing interests can work together to preserve something stunningly beautiful, rich in culture, rich in food, rich in good people. I cannot overemphasize the beauty of the Islands, the ocean, and the abundance of natural nutritious food. The Haida know they have title but the Agreement they have with the governments allows them to co-exist without either party having to expend millions of dollars to prove they have title. Canada should take this as an example of how to engage with Aboriginal people in all areas.

WHAT IF THE COURT SAYS THE HOUSE IS YOURS? CAN YOU TAKE IT BACK?

1993

Xat'súll First Nation joins other Northern
Secwepemc Nations in B.C. Treaty Process

2009

Custom Election Code stabilizes band leadership

2016

Secwepemc Nations reach Stage 5 of the process,
working toward a Final Agreement

Chapter Ten

Realities of Life on the Rez

THE XAT'SÚLL COMMUNITY TODAY

Present Day

JUST LIKE OTHER Aboriginal communities across Canada, Xat'súll sometimes was badly bent but never completely broken. We still have many of the social problems that poverty brings. Very little of our revenue comes from outside the funding agencies such as the Department of Indian Affairs. That means we still do not make the decisions that govern our lives. We are still fighting to be independent and have meaningful participation in the decision-making of our territories. We continue to stand on the shoulders of our ancestors and continue to fight for our rightful place in society.

Our community passed a Custom Election Code in 2009 which replaced the way elections are held under the Indian Act. The change, however, had to be approved by the Department of Indian Affairs. The Custom Election Code we use isn't much different than the one under the Indian Act and is not the traditional way that our people governed ourselves. It is a Custom Election Code that is acceptable to the Department of Indian Affairs and the other non-Aboriginal governing bodies. They make it look like we are self-governing but in reality we are not. We still have to go to the Department of Indian Affairs for approval. The one thing it did do was stabilize the government so there was continuity instead of a new band council every two years.

Under the Indian Act, elections were scheduled for every two years. Because the Human Rights Act did not apply until recently there are stories in a few places where, when a new chief got elected, the entire staff was fired. Some staff knew to pack up their things and leave if a certain person was elected. Usually it took at least two years for a new chief to get to know the ins and outs of being chief. If they tried to start a new project it would usually fall by the wayside if a new council was elected, even if it was a great project. This Department of Indian Affairs system further ensured that nothing positive ever took place. Now things have changed and Aboriginal groups are trying to stabilize their governments. We still, however, face outside interference that prevents many tribes from putting into place something that would work for them.

THE FIRST PART of the twentieth century was marked by continuing efforts to assimilate the Aboriginal people. However, the Aboriginal people adapted to the changing social conditions and began building governance and economic capacity. The governments of Canada eventually came to recognize that it must change its way of dealing with Aboriginal people. The second part of the twentieth century saw movement in response to the Aboriginal people's never-ending struggle to fight the injustice imposed on them.

The solutions for the diverse Aboriginal communities across Canada will be different. As an example, in 1993, Xat'súll First Nation joined together with the Canim Lake, Canoe Creek, and Williams Lake Indian Bands in the B.C. Treaty Process, as a single First Nation called the Northern Secwepemc te Qelmucw or NStQ. We are currently at Stage 5 of the process, working toward a Final Agreement. The treaty process is extremely challenging but we have stayed at the table despite the many disappointments and disagreements on how the negotiations have been conducted. Our ancestors wanted treaties as evidenced in the Sir Wilfrid Laurier Memorial and letters from our former chiefs. They knew that we had to come to an agreement with the newcomers because the newcomers are here to stay.

Direction from local community members comes through the Xat'súll Treaty Working Group, which meets at least once a month. On the other hand, Kekewes e Muts provide input from community members based in Vancouver, the Fraser Valley, Kamloops, and Prince George. Because of budget constraints they meet only a few times a year.

The treaty probably will offer a cash settlement, an expanded land base, and increased self-governance or authority. The governments are still doing their best to keep a check on how we govern ourselves. One of the neat things about our NStQ constitution is that part of it is written in Secwepemctsin. The elders say that the English language has too many meanings for one phrase. That is why, when a court case is won, we celebrate and then the government lawyers get to work to "interpret" the words, which can turn out to mean a number of things. In Secwepemctsin when you say something it means one thing and it cannot be interpreted in other ways. It has always been my theory that because we have an oral culture the word had to be solid. Once I realized that the

> To protect ourselves from "interpretation" our constitution will partly be written in Secwepemctsin.

stories were told over and over again because of our oral history, I remember thinking, "That is why I heard it so many times." I remember reading in one of my history classes something a fur trader said: "The Indians are starting to pick up some of the bad habits of our men. They lie sometimes." I guess the expression *Honest Injun* was based on Aboriginal people who had yet to learn to be untruthful. And so to protect ourselves from "interpretation" our constitution will partly be written in Secwepemctsin.

NStQ negotiators are also pursuing resource revenue sharing, capacity-building initiatives, shared decision-making in natural resource management throughout the traditional territory, and treaty-protected economic measures.

The people of Xat'súll view the B.C. treaty process as one of the options in reclaiming our place as a thriving Secwepemc community. Many are not happy with the treaty process and this was evidenced by the vote to move into Stage 5 this past April. There was not an overwhelming vote to move on and in some communities the vote barely passed. There has to be a return and commitment to the nineteen principles that were put forward to guide the negotiations. Aboriginal people were eager to negotiate at an even negotiating table. Turns out that is not what it is and the government needs to determine whether they want to lose in court or negotiate justly and fairly with Aboriginal people. The Final Agreement will have to satisfy the majority of community members before it passes. Fifty percent plus one of all eligible voters need to vote in support before the Final Agreement passes. Many improvements are needed at the negotiation table for that to happen.

XAT'SÚLL TODAY STILL occupies two Indian reserves: Soda Creek Reserve #1 and Deep Creek Reserve #2, located along Highway 97 north of the city of Williams Lake, British Columbia, and home to almost half of the community's membership.

The Deep Creek Reserve, comprising 1,662 hectares (4,105 acres) is about twenty-seven kilometres north of Williams Lake on the Cariboo plateau, and has now become the main residential and governmental centre of Xat'súll. The reserve follows the course of Deep Creek (also known as Hawkes Creek) from the Westcoast Road in the south to the intersection of Highway 97 and Mountain House Road in the north. Mountain House Road is a gravelled provincial highway that bisects the reserve. About half the Deep Creek Reserve is wooded. The other half has been converted to hay fields. Soil and climatic conditions restrict the use of reserve lands for other crops.

The Soda Creek Reserve, comprising 431 hectares (1,065 acres), is about thirteen kilometres north of the Deep Creek Reserve and forty kilometres north of Williams Lake. This site has been occupied for more than four thousand years.

The Soda Creek Reserve occupies a series of benches above the Fraser River on the east side of Highway 97. The reserve is strategically located at the northern end of a canyon. The first section navigable by steamboats of the Fraser River north of Yale begins at Soda Creek. The Soda Creek Reserve has excellent dip-net salmon fishing sites and good soil for hay and vegetable crops. Because the reserve is located in a canyon, it experiences high summer temperatures and an extended growing season.

However, due to its small area, the Soda Creek Reserve is of limited future use to the community. Landslides have further limited the use and safety of reserve land. As a result, the population of the Soda Creek Reserve has declined over the past two decades. I was at our local store in the community years ago and I was having a conversation with some non-Aboriginal people about the landslide at Soda Creek. A big part of our community was shifting and sliding into the Fraser River. We eventually had to move houses or abandon them out of our main village. A newcomer said to me, "Why did your people pick those lands? You should have picked better lands!" It was similar to another remark made to someone in our community: "Why don't you go back to where you came from!" The ignorance of some newcomers about Aboriginal people and their place in Canada sometimes astounds me.

MOST COMMUNITY SERVICES and facilities are located on the Deep Creek Reserve, including Soda Creek Band administration office, Xat'súll Treaty Office, health centre, community hall, community mail boxes, garbage pickup, and workshop and storage yard. In addition to Deep Creek's health centre, Nenqayni Wellness Treatment Centre offers accredited drug and alcohol addiction treatment programs to adults and youths. Cellphone service to the Deep Creek Reserve began recently, in the past three years. High-speed Internet serves band offices and is also available to residences for a moderate installation cost. Emergency telephone service (911) is also available. Both reserves have local telephone service to Williams Lake. Ironically however, long-distance charges apply to a telephone call between Deep Creek Reserve and Soda Creek Reserve, a distance of less than ten kilometres. Although the Canadian Pacific Railway runs through the reserve, there is no siding or other rail access. Also a natural gas pipeline runs through the reserve but no natural gas service is available on-reserve.

MY COMMUNITY WAS on a boil-water advisory for probably ten years. It's funny that the government blamed our water problems on the beaver. They said there were too many around. We have had beavers in and around our community right from the beginning and we never had anything but good-quality water. Beavers are a natural part of the environment.

I believe our water was contaminated by a paving outfit that set up above our community at Deep Creek, which dumped its waste into the water of the stream where we draw our drinking water. We also have too many cattle in the area whose waste goes into the water. These are not natural contaminants, but the powers that be do not want to acknowledge the real problems because of the financial consequences – so they blame the poor beavers. Common sense goes out of the window when money is involved.

We finally managed to get the Department of Indian Affairs to put in a water system but many other Aboriginal communities are still suffering. Human Rights Watch released a report in June 2016 pointing out that Canada has access to 18 percent of the world's fresh water and is among the world's wealthiest countries, but water quality in dozens of First Nation communities is putting the health of those communities at risk. The report states, "The water supplied to many First Nation communities on lands known as reserves is contaminated, hard to access, or at risk due to faulty treatment systems. The government regulates water quality for off-reserve communities, but has no binding regulations for water on First Nation reserves."

ALTHOUGH COLONIZATION AND a changing economy have placed huge strains on Xat'súll's traditional use of its territory, our people remain strongly attached to the land. Almost every family at Soda Creek and Deep Creek still depends heavily on salmon, game, and indigenous berries and plants for our diet and will travel as far as Quesnel Lake, Cariboo River, Ghost Lake, and Horsefly Lake to harvest these resources. Xat'súll is re-establishing its role as stewards in our territory.

WHAT DO YOU NEED TO FIX YOUR HOUSE
NOW THAT IT'S YOURS AGAIN? WHAT
CAN NEWCOMERS DO TO HELP?

1996

Royal Commission on Aboriginal Peoples Report
calls for a commission to hear stories of those
affected by Indian residential schools

2015

Truth and Reconciliation Commission releases its
final report

2017

Newcomers observe 150 years since
Confederation

The Tilting of Power Back to First Nations

A DUTY TO CONSULT

The Future

OVER THE YEARS, THERE have been royal commissions concerning Indians, justice inquiries, studies, investigations, and in 1996 the final report on the Royal Commission on Aboriginal Peoples was released. That cost $58 million and came with great recommendations. Sadly nothing has really changed for many Aboriginal communities. A lot of money has been spent. Lawyers and consultants have become wealthy. But the government-funded projects were basically "industries with no product." Aboriginal people continue to keep thousands of non-Aboriginal people employed and wealthy. Most Aboriginal people, however, remain in Third World conditions in a land that once belonged entirely to us. I have to question whether change is really wanted.

MANY NEWCOMERS ERRONEOUSLY BELIEVE Aboriginal people have something genetically wrong with them. They do not understand that *any human* would have the same social problems if treated in the same way. Medieval Europe had similar experiences and responses such as rampant alcoholism, social instability, cultural and moral breakdown, spiritual rejection as well as profound mental and emotional withdrawal following the trauma of hundreds of years of plagues. For the past five hundred years, entire Aboriginal nations have been continuously traumatized by massive numbers of deaths from disease, expulsion from their homelands, loss of self-sufficiency, removal of children from their homes, assimilation tactics, and incarceration in prisons and residential schools. The trauma of colonialism is still with us today.

COMPARISON WITH EUROPEAN EXPERIENCES during and after the plagues helps to illustrate that once traumatic events stop for a sufficient length of time – at least forty years – socio-cultural reconstruction and healing can – *will* – begin. After a traumatic period ended, Europeans could go back to their "roots" as their cultural memory remained intact through written records. During the thirty or forty years between major plagues, Europeans were able to experience gradual reconstruction of social order and people were able to repopulate. In most cases they did not become dispossessed of their lands or oppressed by other nations. In the Americas cultural identity was shattered, which prolonged the recovery process. Aboriginal people were unable to reconstruct their societies or repopulate because epidemics hit every seven to fourteen years. This did not allow enough time for recovery. Aboriginal people still have not had the forty-year period needed to start recovery.

> "I have no respect for a society that will crush a man and then criticize him for not being able to stand up under the weight."

I have always said that if you took any population in the world and subjected it to the same conditions that Aboriginal people have endured, it would end up with the same social problems. I was pleased to see that research into this proved correct. Research into postcolonial trauma is under investigation in Australia, South Africa, Ecuador, and among indigenous people around the world. In Canada, the Aboriginal Healing Foundation Research Series reports: "Death, disease, suffering, and cultural genocide have become the deep-rooted painful memories of Aboriginal people. These memories have riveted Aboriginal peoples into spiritual and emotional positions of loss and grief."

When the Truth and Reconciliation Commission final report was published in 2015, some people objected to use of the term *cultural genocide*. That really disturbed me. If not *genocide* then what? Is one group of people's pain greater than another's? Is there a scale of suffering that we can use to measure the pain? How many need to die before it counts as genocide? How do you determine whose experience was worse? Suffice it to say that Aboriginal people are trying to rebuild badly cracked but not completely broken communities.

My point in all of this is that we do not have these social problems in Aboriginal communities today because we are Aboriginal. It is because we are human, and we have experienced traumas. I have used Malcolm X's quote many times as a response when people so quickly condemn Aboriginal people for supposed weaknesses. He said, "I have no respect for a society that will crush a man and then criticize him for not being able to stand up under the weight."

It is so unfortunate that these attitudes are lacking. A foundation of mutual respect and dignity could have been built between newcomers and Aboriginal people from the beginning. These attitudes were not there then. Even today these attitudes are lacking. When Aboriginal issues are discussed on the radio or television someone almost always phones in saying something like, "You Indians are lucky and should be happy that we look after you and that our tax dollars support you." No. That is not true. Had it not been for the Aboriginal people cultivating and nurturing their territories to richness, the resources that so many depend upon would not be there. Had it not been for the individual freedoms that through us were introduced to the rest of the world, many would still be subjects of monarchs. Had it not been for the Aboriginal culture of sharing, the newcomers would not have been able to get established in this country as soon as they did. The fact is that the newcomers are the ones who are lucky and it is the resources of the approximately sixty-seven different tribes in Canada that support their lifestyle.

There is no denying that there is fear among the newcomers. Many are worried about losing their private property. I have heard a number of Aboriginal people tell the newcomers, "We do not want to do to you what you did to us." On the other hand, the Aboriginal position has to be understood. As Bill has said many times, "We are not looking for a bigger cell with a better view in a federal prison. We want to bust out of this prison and achieve freedom."

Despite all the oppression of Aboriginal people I still believe in the basic decency of all human beings. I know that the long, hard fight for survival has made us stronger and wiser. We have learned to manoeuvre in the minefields and are almost to the other side.

WHEN PRIME MINISTER JUSTIN TRUDEAU put together his Cabinet in 2015, it was equally split between men and women. When asked "Why?" his simple response was, "Because it's 2015." I applaud Mr. Trudeau for recognizing that women must be respected.

To me this indicates a society that is maturing. I also applaud Trudeau for stating in all the mandate letters to his Cabinet, "No relationship is more important to me and to Canada than the one with Indigenous Peoples." I applaud Trudeau for putting Aboriginal people front and centre in his government. Aboriginal people are making definite headway. No longer are we "out of sight, out of mind," and people are becoming aware of our fight and starting to understand the issues.

When the Truth and Reconciliation Commission concluded its event in Vancouver in September 2013, a march was planned in solidarity with all former residential school sufferers. I was not in Vancouver at the time but I saw on the news that approximately seventy thousand people, mostly non-Native, turned out to walk in the pouring rain. There were more attendees in the march than in the popular annual Vancouver Sun Run. It made my heart swell. It also proved to me that if people are provided with the proper information and understanding we can work together to build a Canada that works for everyone. However, seventy thousand people do not make a nation. I am also old enough to know that government promises and politicians come and go, so we need to go beyond just the politicians. Without the understanding, education, and co-operation of all Canadians we will not achieve the Canada we all want without further conflict.

This country is an attraction to the entire world and is a lamplight of freedom and opportunity that still remains denied to those who originally owned it "lock, stock, and barrel." The newcomers to Canada will be celebrating 150 years since Confederation in 2017 whereas my people have been here for thousands of years. As a citizen of the Secwepemc and Carrier Nations, I hope that in the not-too-distant future I too can also proudly call myself Canadian.

We have a new country to build with the inclusion of all, not the exclusion of some. It is time to move out of the Dark Ages of Canada. If this happens, we all win, and in that equation, Canada wins.

NOTES

THROUGHOUT THE BOOK I refer to the conflict between Natives and non-Natives as "Native-newcomer relations," using the word *newcomers* to refer not only to the explorers of European heritage who made first contact with the Aboriginal peoples of Canada, but also their descendants and others of non-Aboriginal heritage who live in Canada today.

FOREWORD

Part of this foreword appeared as an article in Postmedia newspapers on October 21, 2008. Thanks to the editors there. As stated in the foreword, the name *Hemas Kla-Lee-Lee-Kla* means "the chief who is always there to help" and "the first rank among the Eagles."

PREFACE

My grandmother, or Gram as I called her, was Sarah Sam (née Baptiste). She was born in 1896 and lived to the age of 101, dying when I was in my forties, after I had returned home to the community.

INTRODUCTION

Linguist Germaine Warkentin sums it up in the introduction to her anthology *Canadian Exploration Literature*: "for in poring over the narratives of the people who were living at that time and place it is we who become the explorers." Warkentin points out a few contradictions that are prime examples. One of them is, "A world seemingly without women is revealed as full of them."

It was a papal bull issued by Pope Alexander VI on May 4, 1493, that declared "the Catholic faith and the Christian religion be exalted and be everywhere increased and spread, that the health of souls be cared for and that barbarous nations be overthrown and brought to the faith itself."

I write about the inquiry that the tribes in our area of Williams Lake demanded be convened in the 1980s. The justice system is a glaring example of the inequalities Aboriginal people experience in Canada today. Although they make up only four percent of the population, Aboriginal women represent 35.5 percent of all incarcerated women while Aboriginal men represent 24.1 percent of all men in custody, states Public Safety Canada's 2015 Corrections and Conditional Release Statistical Overview.

Of course some members of our community had figured out how to "work" the justice system. As I write in my first book, *They Called Me Number One*, Oscar Williams from Sugar Cane, like so many of our people, spent a good deal of time in prison. At one court hearing, Oscar was sentenced to nine months in prison. He told the judge, "I can do that standing on my head!" So the judge added another three months, giving Oscar "time to get back on his feet." Oscar went to prison so many times that he learned the ins and outs of the justice system and started to defend himself in court. He became quite good at it and was a thorn in the side of the Royal Canadian Mounted Police in Williams Lake. They would convict him of something, and he would manage to appeal the sentence and be back in Williams Lake in no time.

Growing up in Deep Creek it was not unusual for my brothers and uncles all of a sudden to jump up and bolt out the back door into the bush or quickly run upstairs to hide. We have a long driveway and could see any car coming long before it got to our house. Not many cars came down our driveway so the noise of an approaching car was picked up right away. If it was an RCMP vehicle, my brothers and uncles disappeared. It was not because they were criminals. They were peaceful people yet every one of them except my grandmother had a criminal record.

CHAPTER ONE
INDIAN GIVERS

Radiocarbon dating of artifacts found in the Old Crow River Basin, Yukon, shows human habitation in Canada goes back to the late Pleistocene. These artifacts defeat the concept of *terra nullius*, which states that Columbus, Cabot, and other European explorers claimed land on the basis that it was devoid of anything, let alone "civilized" society. Land the newcomers saw as a new frontier is, in fact, land that Aboriginal cultures have developed for their use in many ways. Discovery and conquest did not extinguish Aboriginal right to these lands.

Historians document many of the early cotton cloths that are found buried in the deserts of Peru, Bolivia, and Chile. It is believed that the pre-Inca and Inca Nations along the coastal areas of Peru were the first to grow cotton. It then spread to other Aboriginal peoples in South and North America.

Archeologists have found trade goods all across the Americas: obsidian, a black volcanic glass from the central and northern interior of British Columbia, has been found as far away as Prince Rupert on the north coast and Ucluelet on Vancouver Island; pipestone, the hard red clay used for tobacco pipes originating in southwestern Minnesota, important for pipes smoked at rituals and ceremonies, has been found at sites in the upper Midwest and along lakes and river routes in all parts of what is now Canada.

All the discussion of sharing food in this chapter may remind readers of the Puritans and the traditional stories around Thanksgiving. Some Aboriginal people do not celebrate Thanksgiving but view it as a national day of mourning. Thanksgiving to many Aboriginal people marks the beginning of the death of millions of Aboriginal people. Myself, though, I love turkey and I love family being around. There are usually a few welcome strays who attend our dinners as well. I take the opportunity to educate those who don't know about the many foods we enjoy and where they came from. The classic Thanksgiving dinner – turkey, potatoes, cranberries, pecan (pie), pumpkin (pie) were all unknown before Europeans and others came to the Americas. The newcomers may have adopted Thanksgiving from the Aboriginal people but they did not celebrate it as seriously as the Aboriginal peoples. For example, instead of one day a year, the Iroquois had "Thanksgiving Ceremonies" which lasted for days at different times of the year. The Iroquois ceremony was an expression of gratitude for the sun, the winds, the rain, the earth, and everything that grows. The Six Nations have thirteen ongoing ceremonies of thanksgiving per year.

In relation to trade between Aboriginal peoples, anthropologists James Teit and Franz Boas wrote in *The Jesup North Pacific Expedition* of 1909: "One division of the Secwepemc Nation, the Cañon division [who lived in the Farewell Canyon], specialized in salmon fishing, the preparation of oil, and trading. Trade occurred with the Tsilhqot'in (Chilcotin) Nation because they were proficient hunters and trappers. The Cañon division of the Secwepemc received some woven goat's-hair blankets and belts, bales of dressed marmot skins, rabbit-skin robes, and snowshoes in exchange for dried salmon and salmon oil, woven baskets, paint, and in later days, horses."

In one of my history classes I remember reading the journals of someone who took some of the first Aboriginal people to Europe a few hundred years ago. They recorded what the Aboriginal people had to say about life in Europe. The Aboriginal people, for the first time in their lives, witnessed the difference between rich and poor. This was a new concept to them. They saw on the streets homeless people who were begging for food and then they saw the castles and wealth of the leaders of that land.

The Aboriginal people thought for sure that the leaders in those European countries would be killed because that is what would happen to irresponsible leaders in their nations. Most Aboriginal nations had a worldview that placed social concerns and the environment at the centre of everything. The leaders in their nations were responsible for making sure everyone was taken care of and the resources were used but respected. It was not a utopian life but everyone had a role to fill. If times were hard everyone suffered and if times were good, every one benefitted.

CHAPTER TWO
THE TILTING OF POWERS

Further to the discussion of trade between Natives and newcomers, on the Northwest Coast, after Captain Cook and his crew arrived in this country in 1778, they developed trade relationships up and down the coast. Sea-otter pelts were provided to the European traders. It was one of the early mutually beneficial exchanges.

In discussing the Iroquois Confederacy, I referred to the Penner Report, the 1983 report of the House of Commons Special Committee on Indian Self-Government. According to that report, the Iroquois (as they were known by the French) or Six Nations (as the English called them) or the Haudenosaunee (*People of the Longhouse*, as they called themselves) have a formalized constitution, which is recited every five years by elders who have committed it to memory. It provides for a democratic system in which each extended family selects a senior female leader and a senior male leader to speak on its behalf in respective councils. Debates on matters of common concern are held according to strict rules that allow consensus to be reached in an efficient manner, thus ensuring that the community remains unified. A code of laws, generally expressed in positive admonitions rather than negative prohibitions, governs both official and civil behaviour. Laws are passed by a bicameral legislature, made up of senior and junior houses. A council of elders oversees the general course of affairs. Since officials are chosen from each extended family, the system is called "hereditary." While the commonly held belief is that hereditary chiefs hold dictatorial powers, these leaders are actually subject to close control by their people and can be removed from office by them.

As background to the discussion of treaties, particularly Treaty 9, in 1984 Pierre Berton unveiled a 1902 land scam by three civil servants who defrauded two Assiniboia bands in southeastern Saskatchewan of 45,000 acres and then profited handsomely by selling parcels of the land. All three were members of Wilfrid Laurier's Liberal government of the day. "No historian has ever discovered this stuff before," Berton said. "I dug into Hansard, into the ministry correspondences in the National Archives, into committee hearing reports at the time ... The strange thing is that the report of the Government commission about the whole deal (in 1915, under Robert Borden's Tory Government) has vanished. I think the Liberals later got rid of it, fast," Berton told the *Globe and Mail* in September 1984.

In relation to Treaty 6, Jacinda remembers a friend telling her that their Cree community understood the "medicine chest" to mean ongoing health care. Instead, the government tries to give them first-aid kits as part of the annual treaty-day ceremonies, which they refuse.

In implementing a policy of starvation to clear the plains, Daschuk reports that in 1887 Sir John A. Macdonald said: "The great aim of our legislation has been to do away with the tribal system and assimilate the Indian people in all respects with the other inhabitants of the Dominion as speedily as they are fit to change."

CHAPTER THREE
CASE STUDY IN COLONIAL CONTACT

Since the newcomers have arrived, new sources of gold have been struck all over the Americas, from California (1849) to Colorado (1859) to

Alaska and Yukon (1896). One of the most famous was in my backyard: the Cariboo gold rush, which began in the late 1850s. Aboriginal people native to the Cariboo were essential to the newcomers, providing them with food, canoes, skills, and knowledge. The relationship, at least at the beginning, was beneficial to both Aboriginals and to newcomers.

Wendy Wickwire explores contact narratives in "To See Ourselves as the Other's Other: Nlaka'pamux Contact Narratives," *Canadian Historical Review* 75, no. 1: 1–20.

For more information about Reserve Commissioner O'Reilly's negotiations with Soda Creek Chief Koe-mu-salz, refer to *Letters of Reserve Commissioner O'Reilly to the Superintendent General of Indian Affairs, Annual Report of the Department of Indian Affairs for the Year 1861* (Canada 1862. 183, 191, 193), cited in Elizabeth Furniss.

CHAPTER FOUR
WORKAROUNDS AND MEMORIALS

Historian Douglas Cole documents that many Natives voluntarily took part in the artifact market of the late 1800s and early 1900s. In 1995, the *Vancouver Sun* reported that "Sometimes the pieces were burned. But missionaries often kept them or sold them." United Church missionary Thomas Crosby had sold more than three hundred artifacts to American museums during his life, but also gave at least seventy artifacts to his offspring, who have made hundreds of thousands of dollars from their sale. "The *Sun* also learned that more than 80 artifacts gathered by Anglican rector Robert Dundas are in the hands of Dundas's great-grandson, a professor in England who makes no bones about wanting millions of dollars for the 150-year-old artifacts."

The remark by Minister for Indian Affairs Frank Oliver in the House of Commons in 1906 is discussed in Robert Irwin's "No Means No: Ermineskin's Resistance to Land Surrender, 1902–1921," *Canadian Journal of Native Studies* 23, no. 1 (2003): 165–83 at 172, citing E. Brian Titley, *A Narrow Vision: Duncan Campbell Scott and the Administration of Indian Affairs in Canada* (Vancouver: University of British Columbia Press, 1986), 21.

To find out more about how Aboriginal nations were divided up into "new" areas by the newcomers for the ease of the Indian agents and others, the film *How a People Live* traces the history of the Gwa'sala-'Nakwaxda'xw Nations, whom the Canadian government forcibly relocated from their traditional territories in British Columbia in 1964. The film tells the story of their reconnection to the land and their journey of healing and the rejuvenation of their community.

The Indian agent was the hated authority for Aboriginal people throughout the dark years of assimilation policy; then in 1969 the government decided to withdraw Indian agents from reserves. They may have been considered "officially" removed from the reserves but they are still there, just in a different form. As long as the Department of Indian Affairs exists there will always be Indian agents. Later there were others who came into the reserve wanting us to carry out their racist policies. In the 1990s Councillor Dave Pop and I (as chief) were in a meeting with a fisheries agent. He wanted us to give out fishing licences to our people. We had no involvement or knowledge that this was taking place. He showed us what we needed to fill out and then handed the paperwork to us. I took the book and threw it in the garbage by the desk where we were sitting. I shocked the fisheries guy and he later complained to a neighbouring Aboriginal community about my actions. We had never used fishing licences. People knew their rights and didn't need a piece of paper telling them what they could harvest to feed their family. We had our traditional fishing spots that we patrolled and if others were fishing there who shouldn't be, our community members kicked them out. I did give out one licence and that was to John Phillips. John was a member of our community but did not have Indian status. According to newcomer law only status Indians could legally fish for food. John had as much right to catch fish as anyone in the community. I let the fisheries agent know that I gave John a licence and that if he tried to charge him the whole community would be backing John. No charges were ever laid against John for fishing. Under Bill C-31 he later acquired his status.

CHAPTER FIVE

INCREASING CONTAINMENT AND REPRESSION

The pass system is well described in F. Laurie Barron's "The Indian Pass System in the Canadian West, 1882–1935," *Prairie Forum* 13, no. 1 (1988): 25–42. Alex Williams's film on the subject, *The Pass System* (2015), also shares many first-hand accounts through interviews and archival footage.

CHAPTER SIX
POLITICAL ACTION RENEWS

The 1948 parliamentary committee recommendation on the Aboriginal vote is described well in an article on Expanding the Franchise written by Elections Canada for Historica.ca. The article explains that although the Inuit were given the vote in the same year the recommendations were made, First Nations refused the vote because the government required them "to give up the tax exemptions that had been a part of their treaty rights for so long ... Finally, in 1960, the government of John Diefenbaker extended the vote unconditionally to the First Nations."

CHAPTER SEVEN
ABORIGINAL LEADERS AND FIRST MINISTERS

Anyone who wants to look further into the dynamics of the March 1983 constitutional conference should view the two National Film Board documentaries *Dancing Around the Table, Parts One and Two,* filmed by Maurice Bulbulian and crew. The films feature Ethel Pearson in traditional territory.

CHAPTER EIGHT
THE INDIAN ACT AND INDIAN BAND GOVERNANCE

In discussing the Oka Crisis, I relied on reports in the *Huffington Post,* which on July 7, 2015, reported: "Native activists, artists, and professors say while it's difficult to draw direct links, the Oka uprising in 1990 inspired First Nations movements across the country such as the Idle No More protests in 2012 and the ever-increasing calls for a federal inquiry into missing and murdered Aboriginal women." The article quotes University of Ottawa professor Marcelo Saavedra-Vargas, who called the Oka Crisis "an awakening" heard around the world. "I can tell you – from my own experience – that the indigenous social movements in Bolivia, which ended up bringing an indigenous person to the presidency, were also inspired by the Oka events," he said in an interview. Saavedra-Vargas added that at powwows and other celebrations around the continent, "you can always meet Mohawk Warriors talking about how they are proud of what happened. They keep the memory alive."

In the same article, the *Huffington Post* also reported: "The 1990 events led to the Royal Commission of Aboriginal Peoples, which helped usher in new agreements between Natives and non-Natives such as the resource-sharing deal in 2002 called the Paix des Braves (Peace of the Braves) between the Quebec government and the Grand Council of the Crees. Alanis Obomsawin, an award-winning filmmaker who made a much-praised documentary about the conflict called *Kanehsatake: 270 Years of Resistance*, said the events of 1990 inspired Native people across the country and raised awareness among Canadians regarding land claims."

CHAPTER NINE
RE-ESTABLISHING ABORIGINAL RIGHTS
Statements by Perry Bellegarde and Alan Young were reported in an article in the *Globe and Mail* written by Gloria Galloway and published May 13, 2016.

CHAPTER TEN
REALITIES OF LIFE ON THE REZ
Xat'súll First Nation operates a national-award-winning heritage village set on the banks of the Upper Fraser River. Daily tours and programs include time spent visiting with our elders. xatsullheritagevillage.com.

CONCLUSION
Even though the residential schools have been closed, the damage continues. Two great videos about this are Helen Haig-Brown's *My Legacy* and Lisa Jackson's *Hidden Legacies*. The videos focus on the younger generation and how the schools affected them even if they may not have attended them.

Further Reading

APTN. "Mohawk Code Talkers Honoured in Akwasasne Ceremony," May 29, 2016.

Assembly of First Nations. *Reclaiming Our Nationhood, Strengthening Our Heritage: Report to the Royal Commission on Aboriginal Peoples.* Ottawa: Assembly of First Nations, 1993.

Barron, F. Laurie. "The Indian Pass System in the Canadian West, 1882–1935," *Prairie Forum* 13.1 (1988): 25-42.

Bryce, Peter Henderson. *The Story of a National Crime. An Appeal for Justice to the Indians of Canada. The Wards of the Nation, Our Allies in the Revolutionary War, Our Brothers-in-Arms in the Great War.* Ottawa: James Hope and Sons, 1922.

Bulbulian, Maurice, director. *Dancing Around the Table*, Part One. Montreal: National Film Board of Canada, 1987. 57 min.

Bulbulian, Maurice, director. *Dancing Around the Table*, Part Two. Montreal: National Film Board of Canada, 1987. 50 min.

Cardinal, Harold. *The Unjust Society: A Call for Radical Changes in Aboriginal Policy, Rights, Education, Social Programs, and Economic Development.* Vancouver: Douglas and McIntyre, 1969, 1999.

Carter, Sarah. *Lost Harvests: Prairie Indian Reserve Farmers and Government Policy.* Montreal: McGill-Queen's, 1990.

Chrisjohn, Roland D., Tanya Wasacase, Lisa Nussey, Andrea Smith, Marc Legault, Pierre Loiselle, and Mathieu Bourgeois. "Genocide and Indian Residential Schooling: The Past Is Present." In R.D. Wiggers and A.L. Griffiths, eds. *Canada and International Humanitarian Law: Peacekeeping and War Crimes in the Modern Era.* Halifax: Dalhousie University Press, 2002.

Coulthard, Glen Sean. *Red Skin, White Masks: Rejecting the Colonial Politics of Recognition.* Minneapolis: University of Minnesota Press, 2014.

Daschuk, James William. *Clearing the Plains: Disease, Politics of Starvation, and the Loss of Aboriginal Life.* Regina: University of Regina Press, 2013.

Dillehay, Thomas D. *The Settlement of the Americas: A New Prehistory.* New York: Basic Books, 2000.

Duff, Wilson. *The Indian History of British Columbia: The Impact of the White Man.* Victoria: Royal British Columbia Museum, 1997.

Federal Court of Canada. *Bear v. Canada (Attorney General)* (T.D.), [2002] 2 F.C. 356 (2001).

Fournier, Suzanne, and Ernie Crey. *Stolen from Our Embrace: The Abduction of First Nations Children and the Restoration of Aboriginal Communities.* Vancouver: Douglas and McIntyre, 1998.

Furniss, Elizabeth. *The Burden of History: Colonialism and the Frontier Myth in a Rural Canadian Community.* Vancouver: University of British Columbia Press, 1999. n48.

Gallagher, Bill. *Resource Rulers: Fortune and Folly on Canada's Road to Resources.* Waterloo, ON: Self-published, 2012.

George, Chief Dan. "My Very Good Dear Friends ..." In Waubageshig, ed. *The Only Good Indian,* rev. ed. Don Mills, ON: NewPress, 1974. 184–88.

Haig-Brown, Celia. *Resistance and Renewal: Surviving the Indian Residential School.* Vancouver: Tillicum Library, 1988; Arsenal Pulp, 1998.

Harris, Cole. *Making Native Space Colonialism, Resistance, and Reserves in British Columbia.* Vancouver: University of British Columbia Press, 1986.

Haynes, Gary. *The Early Settlement of North America: The Clovis Era.* Cambridge University Press, 2005.

Hewson, Edith. *Dunlevey: A Story of the First Cariboo Gold Strike from the Diaries of Alex P. McInnes.* Lillooet, BC: Lillooet Press, 1971.

Hobson, Richmond P. *Grass Beyond the Mountains: Discovering the Last Great Cattle Frontier on the North American Continent.* Toronto: McClelland and Stewart, 1951.

Indian Act, RSC, 1985, c. I-5. laws-lois.justice.gc.ca.

Irwin, Robert. "No Means No: Ermineskin's Resistance to Land Surrender, 1902-1921," *Canadian Journal of Native Studies* 23, no. 1 (2003): 165–83 at 172, citing E. Brian Titley, *A Narrow Vision: Duncan Campbell Scott and the Administration of Indian Affairs in Canada* (Vancouver: University of British Columbia Press, 1986), 21.

Johansen, Bruce E. *Forgotten Founders: How the American Indian Helped Shape Democracy.* Boston: Harvard Common Press, 1982.

Kramer, Pat. *Totem Poles.* Surrey, BC: Heritage House, 1998, 2008.

Lackenbauer, P. Whitney, R. Scott Sheffield, and Craig Leslie Mantle. *Aboriginal Peoples and Military Participation: Canadian and International Perspectives.* Kingston, ON: Canadian Defence Academy Press, 2007.

Lutz, John Sutton. *Makúk: A New History of Aboriginal-White Relations.* Vancouver: University of British Columbia Press, 2008.

Monture, Patricia A. "A Vicious Circle: Child Welfare and First Nations." *Canadian Journal of Women and the Law* 3, no. 1: 1–17.

Moran, Bridget. *Stoney Creek Woman, Sai'k'uz Ts'eke: The Story of Mary John.* Vancouver: Tillicum Library, 1988; Arsenal Pulp, 1997.

Newhouse, David R., Cora J. Voyageur, and Dan Beavon, eds. *Hidden in Plain Sight: Contributions of Aboriginal Peoples to Canadian Identity and Culture.* Toronto: University of Toronto Press, 2007.

Office of the Auditor General of Canada. "Chapter 4: Programs for First Nations on Reserves." In 2011 June Status Report of the Auditor General of Canada. Cat. No. FA1-10/2011/4E-PDF. Minister of Public Works and Government Services Canada. June 2011.

Office of the Auditor General of Canada. "Land Management and Protection on Reserves." In 2009 Fall Status Report of the Auditor General of Canada. Cat. No. FA1-2009/3-0E-PDF. Minister of Public Works and Government Services Canada. November 2009.

One Dead Indian. Directed by Tim Southam. Sienna Films / Park Ex Pictures production; produced by Jennifer Kawaja, Julia Sereny, Kevin Tierney. Thornhill, ON: Mongrel Media, 2006. 90 min.

Ray, Arthur J. *An Illustrated History of Canada's Native People: I Have Lived Here Since the World Began*, rev. ed. Toronto: Key Porter, 2010.

Royal Canadian Mounted Police. Missing and Murdered Aboriginal Women: A National Operational Overview. PS64-115/2014E PDF. Ottawa: RCMP, 2014. 3.

Royal Commission on Aboriginal Peoples. Report of the Royal Commission on Aboriginal Peoples, 5 vols. Ottawa: Government of Canada, Department of Indian Affairs and Northern Development, 1996.

Sellars, Bev. *They Called Me Number One: Secrets and Survival at an Indian Residential School.* Vancouver: Talonbooks, 2013.

Supreme Court of Canada. *Attorney General of Canada v. Lavell*, [1974] S.C.R. 1349.

Supreme Court of Canada. *Calder et al. v. Attorney General of British Columbia*, [1973] S.C.R. 313.

Supreme Court of Canada. *Delgamuukw v. British Columbia*, [1997] 3 S.C.R. 1010.

Supreme Court of Canada. *Guerin v. The Queen*, [1984] 2 S.C.R. 335.

Supreme Court of Canada. *Haida Nation v. British Columbia (Minister of Forests)*, 2004 SCC 73.

Supreme Court of Canada. *R. v. Drybones*, [1970] S.C.R. 282.

Supreme Court of Canada. *R. v. Sparrow*, [1990] 1 S.C.R. 1075.

Supreme Court of Canada. *St. Catharine's Milling and Lumber Co. v. R.* (1887), 13 S.C.R. 577.

Supreme Court of Canada. *Taku River Tlingit First Nation v. British Columbia (Project Assessment Director)*, 2004 SCC 74.

Supreme Court of Canada. *Tsilhqot'in Nation v. British Columbia*, 2014 SCC 44.

Tennant, Paul. *Aboriginal Peoples and Politics: The Indian Land Question in British Columbia, 1849–1989.* Vancouver: University of British Columbia Press, 1990.

Titley, Brian. *A Narrow Vision: Duncan Campbell Scott and the Administration of Indian Affairs in Canada.* Vancouver: University of British Columbia Press, 1986.

Treaties and Historical Research Centre (Canada). The Historical Development of the Indian Act. Ottawa: Treaties and Historical

Research Centre, P.R.E. Group, Indian and Northern Affairs, 1978.

Truth and Reconciliation Commission. *Canada's Residential Schools: The Final Report of the Truth and Reconciliation Commission of Canada.* Montreal: McGill-Queen's University Press, 2015.

Turner, Nancy J. *Plant Technology of First Peoples in British Columbia.* Vancouver: University of British Columbia Press, 1998.

Union of B.C. Indian Chiefs. *Certainty: Canada's Struggle to Extinguish Aboriginal Title.* n.d.

United Nations, General Assembly. United Nations Declaration on the Right of Indigenous Peoples. UN Doc 07-58681. March 2008.

United Nations, Human Rights Council. Twenty-Seventh Session Report of the Special Rapporteur on the Rights of Indigenous Peoples, James Anaya. UN Doc A/HRC/27/52/Add.2. May 7, 2014.

University of British Columbia Faculty of Arts First Nations and Indigenous Studies Program. Indigenous Foundations website. 2009.

Weatherford, Jack. *Indian Givers: How Native Americans Transformed the World.* New York: Three Rivers Press, 2010.

Weatherford, Jack. *Native Roots: How the Indians Enriched America.* New York: Random House, 2010.

Wickwire, Wendy C. "To See Ourselves as the Other's Other: Nlaka'-pamux Contact Narratives," *Canadian Historical Review* 75, no. 1 (1994): 1–20.

Williams, Alex, director. *The Pass System.* Toronto: Tamarack Productions, 2015. 51 min.

Index

1969 White Paper   109–110

Aboriginal contributions   15–16,
    18, 26, 69
Aboriginal medicine
    See health and healing
adoption, forced   xiii, xvi, 19, 25,
    30, 102–103, 111, 162
agriculture   18–20, 57, 176–177
Alaska (US)   76–77
alcohol and drugs   3, 23, 71, 96,
    108, 136, 177–178
    alcoholism (as coping
        mechanism)   183
Alexandria (B.C.)   3, 24, 86, 141
Alkali Lake (B.C.)   141
Allied Tribes of British
    Columbia   78, 88
"All my relations"   17, 169
American Indian
    Movement   110–111
Assembly of First Nations   5, 96,
    122, 163
Aztec   18

Baptiste, Sarah (Gram)
    See Sam, Sarah Baptiste
Barkerville   53
Basford, Ron   112
basic life skills   3, 7, 9, 24, 30,
    36–37, 45, 51, 72, 165

B.C. Treaty Commission   xxii,
    132, 160–161
Beaver Valley   54
Bella Coola (B.C.)   xxv, xxvi,
    xxvii, 46, 98, 167
berries   22, 24, 45–46, 49, 51,
    55, 179
boarding school
    See residential school
Bones, Frank   83
Boone, Daniel (TV show)   25
Bush, George   28

Calder, Frank   101, 125–126,
    149–152, 158
Calder v. British Columbia
    (Attorney General)
    126, 150–152, 158
Canada Pension Plan
    128, 131–133
Canadian centennial (1967)
    71, 102
Canadian Mortgage and Housing
    Corporation   134–136
Canadian Pacific Railway   42, 178
Canim Lake (B.C.)   141, 174
canoe travel   24–26, 51, 69, 83,
    141, 174
Cardinal, Harold   110
Cariboo-Chilcotin (B.C.)   23, 44

Cariboo Indian School *See* St.
    Joseph's Indian Residential
    School (the Mission)
Cariboo Tribal Council 141
Carrier First Nation
    See Dakelh First Nation.
Cartier, Jacques 21
Casey, Barry 134–135
chewing pitch (spruce gum)
    22, 24, 49
chocolate 18–19
Chrétien, Jean 98, 109–110, 152
Chrisjohn, Roland 101–102
Clinton, Bill 28
Cmetem *See* Deep Creek
code talkers 28, 48, 89–90, 134,
    172–173
colonialism xvii, 23, 41, 53, 56, 77,
    138–139, 155
Columbus, Christopher xviii, 30,
    32, 40
Confederation, 1967 xxii, 41–42,
    109, 119, 182, 187
Congress of Aboriginal
    Peoples 118
constitution xviii, xxii, 11, 27–28,
    116–117, 123–124, 153–154,
    156, 158, 175
Constitution Act, 1982 xxii,
    116–118, 124, 126, 153–154, 156
corn 18–20, 24
cotton 20–21
Cree Nation 39, 70, 88–89,
    103, 165
crime and criminal charges xvi,
    8, 28, 58, 62–63, 65, 69–70,
    74–75, 78, 83–86, 90, 96–97,
    101, 104, 111, 113, 178, 186

Dakelh (Carrier) First Nation
    50–51, 53, 76, 141, 187
Davey, R.F. 71

Deep Creek (Cmetem)
    3, 54, 56, 176–179
Department of Indian Affairs
    10, 29, 42, 56, 61–66, 70,
    73–76, 78, 82, 85, 88–89, 95,
    98, 109, 126, 129, 133–142, 145,
    152, 165, 173–174, 178
DeRose, Cecilia 48, 84–86, 165
disease xxiv, 1, 19, 21, 39–41, 58,
    184–185
Doctrine of Discovery 7, 32
Douglas Treaties 38
Drybones, Joseph 97

Ecuador 165, 184
education xxi, 7–10, 58, 65, 71,
    136, 187
    at college and university xviii,
        2–9, 38, 40–41, 46, 61, 65, 96,
        101, 105, 107–108, 124, 132, 175
    at residential school xxiii, 4, 8,
        10, 57–58, 70–73, 78, 83–84,
        90, 94, 96–97, 100–102,
        104–106, 133, 141–143, 176,
        182, 184, 186
    in public school 8, 73
elders xviii, 22–23, 27–29, 38, 41,
    47, 55, 74, 108, 164, 175
elected officials xxi, 42, 60,
    66–68, 77–78, 88, 94,
    109–110, 117–124, 152, 186
enfranchisement
    and loss of Indian status 83
    and war veterans 80, 88–91,
        97, 101
England xvii, xxii, 35, 37, 104,
    123–124

farming and crops
    See agriculture
federal government xv, 65–66,
    90–91, 111–112, 120, 122, 124,
    132–134, 144, 152–153, 158–159

First Nations   xviii, xxi, xxii, xxiii,
    xxiv, 5, 8, 34, 38–39, 42, 49,
    52–53, 82, 96, 99–100, 105,
    122, 145, 153, 159, 161–163, 183
  and justice system   xxii, xxiv,
    6–8, 29–30, 67–68, 75, 88, 97,
    101–102, 113, 123–124, 126,
    130, 132, 149–158, 160–161,
    163, 169, 171, 175–176
  and residential schools   xxiii,
    4, 58, 70–73, 84, 90, 100, 102,
    105–106, 141–142, 186
First Nations Summit   162–163
First World War   89
food   xv, xvi, 3, 16–20, 22, 24,
    33–34, 36, 39, 42, 45–47,
    49–52, 54–55, 57, 69, 103, 153,
    159, 161, 164–168, 170, 177, 179
Forest Lake (B.C.)   49, 51
Fort Alexandria (B.C.)   24
Fort Simpson (B.C.)   24
France   35, 37
Franklin, Benjamin   28
Fraser River   xvi, 24, 47, 49–52,
    54–56, 69, 164–167, 177
  and fishing   51, 54, 167
  canoe travel on   44, 52
Fraser, Simon   1, 23, 25, 44, 51–52
Fraser Valley   47, 175
fur trapping   xv, 142

George III, King   37
Germany   20
Gilbert, Roberta ("Birdie")   22–23
Gitxsan-Wet'suwet'en First
    Nation   97, 153
gold   17–18, 20, 33, 36, 44, 53–55,
    164, 169
Goodyear, Charles   20
Guerin Decision   152–153
guiding and hunting
    24, 38–39, 55
Gustafsen Lake Standoff   144

Haida Gwaii (B.C.)   26, 76,
    169–170
Harcourt, Mike   xxiii
hay cutting   72, 176–177
healing and reconciliation
    182, 185–186
health and healing   5, 16–17, 20,
    22–23, 39, 41, 47, 51, 55, 73,
    108–109, 168
Hemas Kla-Lee-Lee-Kla (Chief
    Bill Wilson)   xiii, xiv, xv,
    xviii, xix, 2–3, 5, 7, 23, 28, 64,
    68–69, 72–73, 82, 97, 110–111,
    113, 117, 128, 130–132, 152,
    156–157, 159–160, 164, 186
horses   143
hospitals and hospitalization
    4–6, 103, 109
human rights   xxi, xxv, 6, 11, 75,
    81, 88, 96–97, 102, 123, 128,
    130, 133, 158, 162–163, 174, 178
Human Rights Act   128, 133, 174

Indian Act, 1878   xv, xxiv, xxv, 8,
    11, 35, 42, 60–68, 70, 73–76,
    78, 81–82, 85, 88, 90–91,
    94–98, 109, 118, 123, 125–126,
    129–131, 133–134, 145, 150, 161,
    173–174
  amendments   131
  and status   5, 10, 63–65, 73, 83,
    89–91, 97–98, 109, 119, 122,
    128, 130–131, 156
Indian agents   64, 70, 74–76,
    82–83, 85, 125, 142
Indian bands   xiii, xviii, 28, 55–56,
    62–64, 67, 71, 74, 77, 83,
    86, 90, 96–99, 118, 129, 133,
    135–137, 140, 145, 152, 164, 172,
    174, 177
Indian status   5, 10, 63–65, 73, 83,
    89–91, 97–98, 109, 119, 122,
    128, 130–131, 156

Industrial Revolution   20–21
Ireland   19
Iroquois Confederacy   28
Italy   19

jail and prison   xvi, 8, 58, 62,
     69–70, 74–75, 84–85, 96–97,
     104, 111, 113, 186
Jay's Treaty   83–84, 105
Johnson, Doreen   106, 141
Johnston, Gladys   88
justice inquiries
     See Report on the Cariboo-
     Chilcotin Justice Inquiry
justice system, and First
     Nations   7, 29–30

Kamloops (B.C.)   26, 47, 76, 86,
     105, 175
Kingcome Inlet (B.C.)   xiv, xvi
Koe-mu-salz, Chief   55–56, 77
Korean War   89, 91

land
     Aboriginal relationship to
          25, 57, 77, 125
language   xvi, xxv, 2, 15, 22, 25–27,
     47–48, 71, 75, 89–90, 175
languages   2, 17, 25–26, 48, 89, 121
     English   xvi, 2–3, 7, 24, 26–27,
          47, 65, 90, 121, 175
     First Nation   xvi, 47, 49, 58,
          162, 175
     French   2–3, 37, 57, 64–65, 121
     sign   25–26, 38, 53
Laurier Memorial   174
Laurier, Sir Wilfrid
     60, 77, 121, 174
laws and policies   xv, xxiii, 4–7,
     48, 61–62, 70–71, 81–85, 88,
     96–97, 102, 112, 123–126, 132,
     138, 151, 155–156, 162

regalia and dancing, restrictions
     against   xvi, xxvi
law school   4–7, 61, 101, 124
lawyers and law firms
     78, 86, 88, 125
leadership   xiii, xiv, 27, 53, 62, 73,
     110–111, 144, 151, 163, 172
Lévesque, René   120–122
liberty   27
Lima (Peru)   17
livestock   58, 69, 72
Logshom, Chief   44, 52

Macdonald, Sir John Alexander
     xv, 41–42, 82
Mackenzie, Alexander   23, 50–52
Mack, Jacinda   xxv, xxvii, 46, 103,
     106–107, 167–168
Mack, Scott   5, 87, 107, 167
Mack, Tony, Jr.   3, 5, 107–108
Marguerite (B.C.)   50
medical care and treatment
     See health and healing
medicines   22, 30, 34, 39, 49
Meso-American cultures   17–18
Miller Thomson LLP   7–8
monarchy   xxii, 7, 32, 38, 70,
     74, 77, 82, 99, 144, 150, 157,
     182–183
Mount Polley   164–165
Musqueam Indian Band   152, 159

national dream   41
Native language
     See languages, First Nations
Nelson, Jay   105
Nemiah Valley   141
Nlaka'pamux   52
non-status Indians   64, 83, 89, 122
Nuxalk First Nation   xxv, xxvii,
     52, 77, 86, 98, 167

Oakalla Prison xvi, 69, 75, 111–113
Ogden, Lawrence 137
Oka Crisis 130, 143–144
Okanagan Nation
    See Silyx Nation
Oliver, Frank 67
oral history xxi, xxii, 3–4, 17–18, 29, 34–35, 50, 52, 55, 68–69, 74, 154, 174–175, 182
Ottawa 26, 112, 117, 119, 121, 124, 139–140

pass system, to leave reserve 82–83
Pearson, Ethel (Pugledee) xvi, 23, 69, 111–112, 120, 131
Peltier, Leonard 111–113
Peru 17–18
physical violence xvii, xviii, xxiv, 10, 37, 41, 46, 89–90, 96, 105, 126, 129, 144, 149, 152, 164, 166, 169, 173–174, 184, 186
plant-based medicines
    See traditional medicines
police See Royal Canadian Mounted Police
politics xxi, 63, 66–68, 78, 91, 94, 101, 117–118, 124, 152, 162, 172–173
    Aboriginal xix, 27, 29, 48, 63, 75, 78, 113, 117, 125, 129
    non-Aboriginal xxi, 42, 60, 66–68, 77–78, 88, 94, 96, 98, 109, 112, 117–124, 145, 152, 163, 186
Pontiac, Chief 37
Pop, David 136
Pope Alexander VI 32
population estimates xxiv, 14, 20, 37, 41–42, 44, 169, 177, 184
potatoes 19–20, 49

potlatch xiii, xiv, xv, xvi, xviii, 24, 60, 67–69, 78, 83, 111–112, 118, 125
prison and jail See jail and prison
Proclamation of property rights
    See Calder v. British Columbia (Attorney General)
punishment for speaking xv, 38, 58, 89–90, 154

Quesnel (B.C.) 49–51, 54, 87, 141, 164, 179

racism and oppression 87
Report on the Cariboo-Chilcotin Justice Inquiry 7
reserves xvii, xxiii, xxiv, 3–4, 10, 39, 45, 54–57, 61–62, 65–67, 70, 72–73, 77, 80–83, 88, 90, 96–97, 105, 110, 129–140, 144–145, 152, 161–162, 165, 169, 176–178
    and Indian status 8, 10, 62
    life xiii, xiv, xvi, xvii, xviii, xxi, 3–5, 9–10, 17, 26, 40, 46–48, 71, 73, 76, 82, 86, 90, 98, 100, 103–109, 124, 129–130, 133–138, 140, 142, 144, 164–166, 173, 176, 178
residential school xxiii, 4, 8, 10, 57–58, 70–73, 78, 83–84, 90, 94, 96–97, 100–102, 104–106, 133, 141–143, 176, 182, 184, 186
resource extraction 17–18, 38, 47, 168–169
rodeo
    See Williams Lake Stampede
rowboats 24–25
Royal Canadian Mounted Police 7, 70, 74–75, 82, 99, 144
Royal Proclamation of 1763 xxii, xxiii, 8, 32, 37, 62, 65, 150
rubber 20–21

Russia   20

Sacagawea   25
salmon   xv, 24, 49–52, 54–55, 57,
     159, 164–167, 177, 179
Sam, Sarah Baptiste (Gram)
     3, 45, 72–74, 84–86, 106,
     108–109, 138, 142
Sam, Walter (*Xp'e7e*, "Ba'ah")   xiii,
     xiv, xv, xvi, 23, 28, 45, 69, 74,
     84–85, 103, 106–108, 111
Second World War
     80, 88–91, 97, 101
Secwepemc language
     47, 49, 58, 175
Secwepemc Nation   14, 22, 24,
     44–45, 47–48, 50–54, 57,
     67, 76–78, 81, 84, 98, 100,
     105–106, 141, 164–165, 172,
     174, 176, 187
See languages, sign   25–26
Sellars, Annie (Baptiste)   73
Sellars, Bev   xviii, xix, 6, 8, 126
   and Chief Bill Wilson   2, 5
   and children   xxv, xxvii, 3, 5,
     46, 87, 98, 103–104, 106–108,
     110, 167–168
   career as chief
     9, 29, 52, 61–62, 141
   environmental activism
     142, 168
   life at Deep Creek   177–178
   university education   xxv, 2–4
Sellars, Leonard (Lenny)   84–85
Sellars, PeeWee (James)   86
Sellars, Teena   168
Senese, Phyllis   4
sharing culture   xv, xxiv, 13,
     17–18, 24, 33–34, 36, 48–49,
     65, 68, 107, 142, 166, 175, 185
Shuswap   *See* Secwepemc
silver   17–18, 20, 91, 120, 166
Silyx Nation   77, 84

Sixties Scoop   37, 46, 94, 102–105
smallpox   23, 39–40, 44
Soda Creek Band
     See Xat'sull Band
Soda Creek (B.C.)   xxi, 3, 14, 16,
     54–56, 65, 73, 76, 83, 98, 139,
     141, 144, 176–179
Songhees First Nation   66
Spain   17, 35
Sparrow case   153
starvation   42, 91, 102, 131
Stemémelt Secwepemc Nation
     Project   105
St. Joseph's Indian Residential
     School   58, 71
Sugar Cane   *See* Williams Lake
     Indian Band
sundance   60, 68–69, 83
Supreme Court of Canada   6–7,
     97, 126, 130, 149–151, 153–156,
     158, 163
Switzerland   19

talking stick   27
taxes   9–10, 168
Teit, James   52
territory   14, 23–25, 34, 38–39,
     47–50, 52–55, 57, 75–77, 81,
     105, 118, 143–144, 150–151,
     154–155, 164, 167, 176, 179
Thompson First Nation
     See Nuxalk First Nation
Tomaah (Indian guide)   44, 53
trade   15, 18, 25–26, 33, 36–37,
     49–51, 53
traditional medicine
     20–23, 49, 164
traplines   *See* fur trapping
travel   10, 139, 179
   by canoe   24–26, 51, 69, 83,
     141, 174
   by Greyhound   100
   by horse   101, 106–107, 143

treaties   xxii, xxiii, 37–39, 54, 65,
     77, 109, 158–160, 174
   in British Columbia   38, 54–55,
     126, 148, 151–152, 158–160
   in Quebec   39, 143, 158
   medicine chest clause   39
   numbered   38–39, 96, 159,
     167, 184
   peace and friendship   37
   today   158
   Treaty 6   39
   Treaty 9   38
treaty process   xxii, 152, 160–161,
     172, 174, 176
tribal council   99, 134, 141, 151,
     158, 160–161
Trudeau, Justin   186
Trudeau, Pierre Elliott   109, 117,
     120–121
Truth and Reconciliation
     Commission of Canada
     182, 185–186
Tsilhqot'in (Chilcotin) Nation
     76, 126, 148, 155–156, 163
     see also Xeni Gwet'in case
Tsimshian   24
tuberculosis   39, 73

United Nations 130
United Nations Declaration on the
     Rights of Indigenous Peoples
     162–163
United States of America   21–23,
     28, 53, 76–77, 83–84, 89,
     103–104, 110–113, 118
university and college
     See education
University of British Columbia
     4, 101
University of Victoria   3, 8
Upper Canada Treaties   38

Vancouver (B.C.)   xiii, xvii, 2–5,
     19, 26, 38, 47, 55, 69, 88, 100,
     152, 159, 164, 175, 186–187

Vancouver Island   xiii, xvii, 2–3,
     26, 38, 55, 69, 159
Victoria (B.C.)   3, 40, 57, 66, 72,
     83, 144
violence against women   99–100
vote   63, 81, 96–98, 100–102, 125,
     162, 176
   federal   81, 101, 125
   provincial   100–101, 125

war veterans   89–91
Washington, George   22
Weatherford, Jack   15
Wells (B.C.)   86
westerns (movies)   35, 89
Wickwire, Wendy   1, 52
Williams, Bryan   6
Williams Lake (B.C.)   4–5, 45, 47,
     52, 56, 67, 71–72, 74, 76, 82,
     84–87, 109, 140–141, 164, 174,
     176–178
Williams Lake Indian Band
     22, 57, 67, 71, 164
Williams Lake Stampede
     85–86
Wilson, Charlie   xvi, 98, 125
Wilson, Chief Bill
     See Hemas Kla-Lee-Lee-Kla
Wilton, David   15
women   xxv, 34–35, 41, 46, 57,
     63, 83, 89, 96–99, 108, 128,
     130–131, 165, 186
   Indian status   3, 35, 63, 83,
     98–99, 111, 130–131
   missing   99
   violence against   99–100

Xat'súll Band   45, 47-58, 76-78,
     99, 172-177, 179, 196,
     208-209, 211
Xeni Gwet'in (Tsilhqot'in) case
     126, 148, 155
Xp'e7e (grandfather)
     See Sam, Walter (Xp'e7e)

Acknowledgements

THANK YOU TO my grandparents, especially my grandmother, for teaching me that another truth existed.

Thank you to elder Cecilia DeRose and my brother-in-law, Chris Wycotte, for their many stories from the oral history of our nation.

Thank you to the many people who contributed to the development of the profiles of the Xat'súll First Nation in Chapter Three and Chapter Ten, including Teena Sellars, Cliff Thorstenson, Donna Dixon, Jacinda Mack, Lindie Jay Mitchell, Lawrence Sellars, Norman Michel, and Ed Baptiste.

Thank you to Chris Arnett and especially to Phinder Dulai for highlighting the What If questions this text poses.

Thanks to Kevin Williams of Talonbooks for believing I had another book in me and encouraging me to write it. Thank you to Les Smith for beautiful layout and design. Thanks to Chloë Filson, Vicki Williams, Greg Gibson, and the whole Talon team for help getting the book to press. I especially would like to thank Ann-Marie Metten without whom this book would not have been completed.

Bill Wilson

BILL WILSON is a politician and administrator born at Comox, British Columbia, on April 6, 1944. He graduated from the University of Victoria with a bachelor of arts in 1970 and from the University of British Columbia with a bachelor of law in 1973. Wilson was the leading theorist in B.C. Aboriginal politics and was influential in every major development. Although initially active in both the Union of B.C. Indian Chiefs and the B.C. Association of Non-Status Indians (BCANSI), he advocated reducing the role of these organizations in favour of a return to unity of all Aboriginal peoples at the level of the traditional Aboriginal tribes or nations. He was founding president of the United Native Nations (1976–1981), the renamed BCANSI which sought support of all B.C. Aboriginal peoples and encouraged tribal political development. In 1982–1983 he was vice-president of the Native Council of Canada, attaining national prominence as its spokesman at the 1983 First Ministers' Conference. He chose not to seek re-election, and returned to his own Kwawkgewlth (Kwakwala) nation to become coordinator of the Musgamagw Tribal Council.